Angel in Tennis Shoes

DEVOTIONALS FOR CHRISTMAS

Jamie Denty

Denty/New Harbor Press
1601 Mt. Rushmore Rd, Ste 3288
Rapid City, SD 57701
www.newharborpress.com

Angel in Tennis Shoes/Jamie Denty —1st ed.
ISBN 978-1-63357-410-6

Cover Art by Erica Boyd

All Scripture quotations are taken from the Holy Bible, King James Version (Public Domain).

Dedicated to
Erin, Eric, and Lowry
You continue to inspire me.

Preface

WHENEVER WE THINK OF Christmas, we think of children. We smile with their excitement throughout the last month of the year. Our own childhood usually gives rise to our happiest memories of the holidays. For a child, then or now, Christmas trees, presents, parties, candy canes, lights, decorations stimulate a snowballing effect toward December 25.

And yet, children, more than anyone else, have a way of cutting through the trappings to the essence of things. Given the chance to experience the true message of Christ's birth, they understand what we adults often forget. If we listen to them and watch them and put away our cynicism, we can discover the true meaning of the season anew. Let us then treat ourselves to Christmas, the gift that keeps on giving throughout the year.

When our children were young, I delighted in the way they expressed themselves. I noted all the cute sayings in their baby books, but the lines stayed in my heart. And so, I found myself not only recording what they said, but how it touched my soul. As my friends told about the expressions of their own children, I identified with them, too. I learned to listen to every child I met. Out of these encounters grew this collection. Once I had grandchildren, I felt as if I had been given a second chance to listen anew.

Divided into four facets of Christmas: Nativity, Gifts, Advent and Epiphany, *Angel in Tennis Shoes: Devotionals for Christmas* offers a variety of anecdotes about the season. While most of these stories evolved out of my own home or those of my friends, the faces and words of the children are universal. Some of these selections were prompted by the experiences of adults who, childlike, also realized the true meaning of Christmas.

Each of these selections first appeared in the pages of *The Press-Sentinel*, the official newspaper in Jesup, Georgia, for more than 150 years. In addition to teaching high school English and journalism for 20 years, I have been a columnist for this newspaper and other publications for more than 50 years.

Nativity

For unto you is born this day in the city of David a Savior, which is Christ the Lord. And this shall be a sign until you: Ye shall find the babe wrapped in swaddling clothes, lying in a manger...Luke 2:11-12

Angel in Tennis Shoes

Peace on earth: good will toward men. Luke 2:14.

IN THE CHRISTMAS PAGEANT, he was an angel in tennis shoes, ragged ones at that. He wore a discarded choir robe, slightly yellowed with age. He said of himself, "I'm a cheap angel. My wings are made of coat hangers covered with gold garland."

During the performance, his voice was childlike as he was, not angelic as he was pretending. He sang, "Peace on earth; good will to men!" And as he knelt in humble adoration before a doll baby in a wooden manger, his face was etched with awe and wonder and all of the hope in the world.

Dressed as an angel, this representative of all children the world over, sings a song reflective of the child's hopes. It is similar to his belief in Santa. He believes in the giver of gifts; he believes it can be a world without wars; he believes he can grow up and not have to fight with a real gun in a real war.

If his hope dies, if his belief is shattered, if adults cease trying to make the world a better place, if no one works for "peace on earth; good will to men," then the Christ Child was born in vain and we celebrate Christmas for naught.

But the Christ Child was born. We still celebrate Christmas. There is still Hope. There is still Belief. Adults still try. And, an angel in tennis shoes still sings with all his heart, "Peace on earth; good will to men."

Almost Wise

...and a little child shall lead them. Isaiah 11:6.

It's almost Christmas time,
    But, I don't have to tell you that,
    You can see it reflected in a child's eyes.
He's almost seven years old,
    Old enough not to believe in Santa,
    Young enough still to want to believe.
He stands almost four feet tall...on tiptoe,
    High enough to look over countertops,
    And wish for this and this and that.
He's almost mastered time-telling,
    By counting days backwards until Christmas,
    Ten, nine, eight...like an astronaut's countdown.
He's almost been a help,
    In decorating the eight-foot tree,
    Only six feet up – as high as his chubby arms can stretch.
He's almost learn to read,
    All of the greeting cards which have come by mail,
    And all the ones on which he's put stamps.

He's almost memorized all the words to
    "Twas the night before Christmas..."
    And "Away in the Manger..."
It's almost time for the annual Christmas pageant,
    The one held out on the church's lawn,
    Under God's stars.
He's almost ready to be a Magi, one of the three,
    In his brother's too-big bathrobe,
    And a cardboard crown.
He's almost confident of his lines,
    About coming from afar
    And adoring the Infant Christ.
It's almost time for him to speak his part,
    He kneels by the manger-crib,
    His gift of myrrh extended.
There's a hush,
    My heart's a flutter
    As my own babe stands so vulnerable before the world.
He almost pauses too long, then ad libs clearly,
    "Happy Birthday, Baby Jesus,
    Thank you for inviting me to your party..."
Oh, to be almost as wise as he!

Pondering

But Mary kept all these things and pondered them in her heart.
Luke 2:19.

Did she ponder about...
   The whole set of pyramiding events that brought her to this place, this night? Did she ponder about an announcement from God; Joseph's faith in God and devotion to her; a king's decree; a tiring trip; too many people; too little room?
Did she reflect about...
   A loving husband, hurting inside because he could do no better? Did she think warmly of this man who made the best possible arrangements that he could for her and the Child, who showed his concern for them as he selected the freshest and cleanest hay?
Or did she wonder about...
   The night – the too still, mysterious night; the star – the too bright, extraordinary star; the animals – the too quiet, accommodating animals sharing their quarters; the music – the too melodious, holy music in the air?
Did she muse, as new mothers always do, about...

Her first born, this beautiful babe? Did she count ten chubby little fingers and ten fat little toes? Did she pet his baby fine hair and gently stroke her finger across the bridge of his tiny nose and down his pudgy cheek: Did she marvel at the miracle of birth?

Did she weigh in her heart...

The unknown future of this infant; her hopes for his achieving his potential; her dreams for his happiness; her prayers for God's guidance; her fears for his safety? Did she wonder what lay ahead for this most unusual child born this most unusual night?

Or did she consider...

The many visitors who came to give tribute; who told of strange sights and happenings? Did she remember the foreigners called Magi, Wise Men, who came later following the star that followed the family wherever it went? Did she remember unrecorded strangers – a small child, a young maid, the stable hand, a merchant late closing his business, a traveler from another town?

Did she speculate about...

Others yet to be who would remember this most important night to her? Did she know that it would become a most important night for peoples the world over? Did she know that this story would be told and sung and painted in countless ways? Did she know that stories would be told on top of stories like "The Little Drummer Boy," "The Littlest Angel," "The Fourth Wise Man?"

Did she realize...

That some 2,000 years later, another little boy, four years old, would ask his mother, "On my birthday, I get presents. On Jesus' birthday, I get presents, too. Is that what Christmas is all about...Jesus giving away his presents?"

But Mary kept all these things, and pondered them in her heart.

Belonging

...My soul magnifies the Lord, and my spirit rejoices in God my Savior. Luke 1:46-47.

A SCRAP OF SOFT blue wool framed her cherubic face and draped gently over her tiny shoulders. But, wisps of baby fine hair escaped the clasp of a barrette and peeked from beneath the blue. A slightly yellowed choir robe hung loosely over the rest of her small frame. And summer's sandals were strapped across her feet.

She entered the well-lit room beside a classmate clad in a plaid bathrobe, a towel tied turban style around his head. With a tight fist, she grasped her head covering under her chin, and in her other arm, she awkwardly carried a fragile bundle wrapped in white.

Her eyes demurely watched her feet as she climbed three steps to the stage and then took her place on a low bench. Her companion, constantly by her side, shoved more than assisted. But finally, the couple clumsily settled into their places beneath a golden cardboard star.

Hesitantly, she tugged at the swaddling cloth around her bundle and whispered a lullaby to the form within. Her escort roughly placed his hand on her shoulder. Leaning forward slightly, she laid a doll in a crude wooden crib filled with pine straw, a make-believe manger.

As if in prayer, she folded her hands and sat ever so still. Sentry-like, the other child stood protectively at her side. And they held this stance firmly as angels sang, shepherds paraded by and wise men knelt. Voices, eyes, and the gold-painted star sparkled with the brilliance of the moment.

Houselights dimmed and the nativity scene actors scampered off. She grabbed her doll by an arm and both her headgear and the babe's blanket fell away. Her eyes danced in step with her feet as she searched out her own parents.

"Mama! Daddy!" She ran into their embrace. "Did you see? I was part of the Christmas story tonight!"

During this holy season, may we, too, feel like a part of the story, not just an onlooker.

The Wonder of It All

For unto us a child is born, unto us a son is given...and his name shall be called Wonderful, Counselor, the mighty God, the everlasting Father, the Prince of Peace. Isaiah 9:6.

EACH CHRISTMASTIDE, PEOPLE PAUSE to remember the wonder of the first Christmas.

...Is there wonder only in the existence of a brilliant star? Or, is it in the fact that some people lifted their eyes to see it? Would I look up?

...Is there wonder only in the angels' serenade to the shepherds? Or is it in the fact that the shepherds heeded the message in song? Would I listen?

...Is there wonder only in the journey of the Wise Men following the star? Or is it in the fact that three men were wise enough to search for its meaning? Am I so wise?

...Is there wonder only in the Virgin Birth? Or, is it in the fact that there was a couple present with whom God would entrust the earthly care of His only Son? Would He so entrust me? Has He?

...Is there wonder only in the acceptance that Christmas really happened, just once, 2,000 years ago? Or is it found in knowing that Christmas can happen every day, every year? Does it happen for me?

I once read that an octogenarian, upon joining the church, exclaimed, "I'm just glad that the Lord didn't think this creaky manger was too old for Him to be born in me!" One is never too old nor too young to experience Christmas first hand, to experience the wonder of Christmas, the miracle of Christmas.

And therein lies the wonder of it all.

And Suddenly

And suddenly there was with the angel a multitude of the heavenly host praising God... Luke 2:13.

"AND SUDDENLY THERE WAS with the angel a multitude of the heavenly host," the narrator read from the scriptures as the crew of young children moved through the vignettes of the Christmas story.

As she read about the angel and the multitude, a snicker rippled across the audience. Puzzled, she turned toward the cherubs in the choir loft. But, lo, not only had the heavenly host failed to materialize, the angel had also disappeared. The narrator tried the cue again. "And suddenly there was with the angel..." Nothing. Snickers gave way to hearty laughter.

Standing on tiptoe and peeking over the high railing of the choir loft, the narrator directed the flock of angels clad in white gowns and gold garland wings to their place on the risers. The youngest bit her lips as her halo slipped from its angelic place encircling her head down over her forehead, headband style. Shakily, the cardboard star arose and the play continued.

Clearing her throat, the narrator began to read again. "And suddenly there was with the angel a multitude of the heavenly host praising God and saying, 'Glory to God in the highest and on earth, peace, good will toward men.'"

For children, Christmas doesn't come suddenly. Ask any child. There are endless days of waiting. And each day sparks unmatched anticipation. After all, when you are a child, birthday parties, whether they be yours or someone else's, are special.

Yet for a child, Christmas frequently ends suddenly. Tucked into bed after a long, exciting day, a child is often overcome by both weariness and a strong sense of sadness because he no longer has anything to look forward to. At least, for the moment, he can't think of anything.

For adults, Christmas doesn't come suddenly either. There are a multitude of chores to accomplish before the big day – trees to trim, cards to mail, gifts to buy, packages to wrap, cakes to bake, parties to attend. There is always something to be done.

But Christmas shouldn't end suddenly either. If it does, then perhaps it wasn't Christmas after all. All the warm, glowing celebration of the Christ Child's birth should be a beginning, not an end. Actually, it is a most appropriate way to begin a new year.

For as the Child "grew in stature and wisdom, in favor with God and man," so, too, should our response be one of growth, of reaching out in the spirit of Christmas, of following the shepherds' lead.

Remember after hearing the angels and kneeling at the manger, the shepherds returned, "glorifying and praising God for all the things that they had heard and seen as it was told unto them."

Memories

...to have these things always in remembrance. II Peter 1:15.

THE CARDBOARD CRÈCHE WAS a last minute purchase, really a last minute thought, years ago. Christmas after Christmas, it was dragged out of storage and set up, in the place of honor under the tree.

The familiar nativity scene came with cut-outs of the Holy Family. Mary, dressed in heavenly blue, smiled motherly at her newborn. Joseph, wearing peasant's garb, stood protectively by his young family. And the Babe, the Infant Babe, rested in a painted bundle of hay. Completing the picture were the animals stabled for the night; the shepherds, afraid, curious, awed; the angel perched in vigil; wise men bearing gifts and the star in brightly painted splendor.

Frayed from being assembled yearly, dog-eared from childish play, this crèche had served its purpose well. It was time, however, to throw it away and buy another to take its place. After all, it only cost a couple of dollars. But to the children, the ragged crèche not only told "The Story," it had become a very real part of their happiest memories.

What to do? Dad took a sheet of plywood and with a jigsaw, he cut out the intricate shapes. Painstakingly, he glued each original piece onto its wooden counterpart. Still today, it is packed away eleven months out of the year. But for one month, one special month, it stands proudly, humbly, telling the Christmas story in a glance.

Think quick! Of all your fondest Christmas memories, how often are material extravagances recalled? More often than not, it is the inexpensive, fragile "crèches" with stories of their own that are remembered best.

Who can explain the mystery of the longevity of this crèche? Is it just an understanding of the message it tells so simply? Or is it the look in a young girl's face as she sets up the three-dimensional picture again? Or is it just an appreciation of a dad's efforts to salvage it from the trash can? Somehow, as the worn-out cardboard crèche stands in front of all of the presents and tells its own story of human love, it embodies the holy love it portrays.

Where Are Mary and Joseph Going?

As the angels were gone away from them into heaven, the shepherds said one to another, Let us go even unto Bethlehem...Luke 2:15.

THE CHURCH WAS STILL, stiller than usual for an evening service. Even the children who normally squirmed in the hard pews snuggled against their parents in anticipation of what was to come. Only the flame of candles in the windows flickered. Christmas Eve.

As the clock chimed the hour, role players took their places in the familiar nativity scene to create a real life crèche. Joseph plumped the straw in the manger. Mary, clad in traditional blue, held the baby close to her breast. One by one, the shepherds came, followed by the bejeweled wise men. The choir took its place in the loft as the heavenly host of angels. And the narrator began to read, "And it came to pass in those days that there went out a decree from Caesar Augustus..."

When the scripture reading concluded, the actors departed leaving the choir to inspire the congregation with the story in song. However, it was too much for one blonde three-year-old. Wide-eyed, she whispered to her mother, "Where did Mary and Joseph go?"

In motherly fashion, Mother put an arm around the child and whispered in her ear, "Shhh..."

But the little girl would not be shushed. She repeated her question, this time louder, loud enough for those around her to hear, "Where did Mary and Joseph go?"

Mother, once again whispering in the child's ear, made it quite clear by both her actions and words that the forthcoming paddling, if she continued to disturb, would be painful indeed.

Momentarily, the youngster was subdued. She sat back in her seat and looked for her father in the choir loft. She tried, really tried, to forget what troubled her and to listen to the music.

But as the choir ended one selection and turned the pages of their songbooks to the next, the question burned in her inquisitive mind as much as the candle would have seared her hand if she had reached out and touched it. She sighed aloud and then answered her own question in a voice loud enough for all – congregation, choir and God – to hear. "I guess they had a meeting to go to."

Face turning every shade of red in the spectrum, Mother yanked the child up and carted her out the back door. With a face the matching shade of red as his wife's, Dad lowered his head and covered his eyes with his hand. Under the guidance of the director, the choir tried to stifle its amusement. The congregation roared. The spell had been broken.

Or, had it?

For the wisdom of a child often supersedes the propriety of adults. Her brief explanation acknowledged that Mother and Dad had probably left her with a sitter more times than she liked while they attended a variety of church and civic affairs by "going to a meeting." It also illustrated her understanding of family. She assumed the mommy and daddy of the baby Jesus also left together "to go to a meeting."

But it says so much more to us. Where did Mary and Joseph go? To a meeting?

Certainly, they did. They traveled at one man's decree to their destination with God's infinite plan for them, and there, in the most unlikely of all places, a stable behind a crowded inn, they met the Christ Child and assumed all the responsibilities thrust upon them to raise the Son of God by God's laws.

And today, we're likewise called "to go to a meeting" with Him. He is always present. It is we who must stand up or kneel down, straighten our priorities as we would our clothes, and move on to this most important meeting with God through the Savior. Christmas Season. Christmas Eve. Christmas Day summons all of us to a meeting.

Where did Mary and Joseph go? To a meeting, of course. And they and the Babe and God Himself wait for us to join them. Let us go even now.

Where Is the Fourth Wise Man?

And lo the star, which they saw in the East, went before them till it came and stood over where the young child was. Matthew 2:9.

HE NIBBLED ON THE end of his homemade wing, unaware of the tinny tinsel woven tightly around the wire shaping it. His freshly laundered robe was already crumpled as he sat on the oak stairs to the stage, which, recently polished, bore scuff marks.

Around him, chaos reigned.

Bathrobe-clad shepherds chased one another around the platform while an angel knocked off the crown of a Wise Man. A pint-sized Mary dragged a baby doll by one leg and the heavenly host wandered aimlessly as mothers pinned, buttoned, adjusted costumes, combed hair, coerced the shy ones and admonished the overactive ones.

But the lone angel sat.

"I gotta go to the bathroom!" blurted out a miniature Magus, dressed in royal blue. He tugged at the director's skirt to emphasize the urgency of his demand.

"Hurry back!" she murmured through a mouthful of pins.

"I'm scared," one of the angels cried as she buried her face into the shoulder of the director, kneeling to adjust a costume.

Pinning up the last hem, the director snapped, "There's nothing to be afraid of. Nothing is going to bite you and the roof isn't going to fall in. Now go to your place!" She gently shoved the child in the general direction of her place on stage.

And still, the angel sat, wing in hand.

"Places everyone!" the director clapped her hands. Taking two by the hand, she led them to their positions and threatened, "Now stand here and don't you dare move!"

She looked around and frowned, "Where's the third Wise Man?"

"He's not back from the bathroom," a chorus of young voices sang.

She shook her head.

Walking around the stage, she physically tugged and pulled and set characters right. With force, she sat Mary on her stool and straightened the swaddling cloth around the doll baby. "Smile," she growled through clenched teeth.

She straightened halos made of Christmas tree garland and wings shaped out of coat hangers. It was then that she noticed an angel was missing.

"Where's the fifth angel?" she inquired of the child next to the vacant spot.

He nodded across the stage to the solitary figure, sitting still on the stairs to the stage.

The director rushed over to the little angel and grabbed him by the hand. "What do you mean not taking your place? How did your wing come off? Never mind, it's curtain time."

The third Wise Man, tugging at his robe, ran back on stage and took his place. The director nodded, then she reshaped the bedraggled wing of the angel. Pulling a big safety pin from a giant pincushion, she spun the child around so that she could mend the broken wing. "Now it's fixed. Tell me this, what were you doing when the rest of us were frantically getting ready?"

"I was trying to do my part," he whispered.

"And just what was that?" she glared.

"You know, where I say, 'God commands: Be still and know that I AM God.'"

A Baby's Low Cry

Jesus wept. John 11:35. *And when he was come near, he beheld the city and wept over it.* Luke 19:41.

THE SUN IS STILL shining as I take my seat in the church for the Christmas Eve service. In looking around, I immediately notice a giant flickering image of a lit candle in a green wreath. This pastel illusion, reflected on the eastern wall across the wide expanse of the sanctuary, has been cast by the setting sun beaming through a brightly colored stained glass window.

Fascinated, I watch this faint mural dancing on the pristine wall of white.

A tall Chrismon tree sparkles as its white lights illumine the glittering Christian symbols adorning the tree. Lit candles glow in every window and line both the altar and choir railings. The minister lights the Christ candle in the Advent wreath. And from this central flame, the individual candles held by members of the congregation will be lit later during the service. And yet, it is the reflected image that stirs my imagination.

The sanctuary is filled almost to capacity. During the service, various members of the congregation read the old familiar

Christmas story from the Bible. And as the sky darkens and the wreath image fades, babies begin to cry, first one, then another. Embarrassed parents hurry them from the sanctuary. But what more appropriate sound is there for a celebration of the birth of the Christ Child than that of an infant's cry? While some in the congregation may have rejoiced that it is not their child so unhappy, many of us want to reach out, to hold, to soothe the hurt.

Yet when we study the Christmas story, none of the gospel writers ever mention the Baby Jesus crying, Mary comforting or Joseph walking an inconsolable babe. Few artists have ever painted a crying Christ Child. Over time, most have always painted a baby smiling or sleeping or looking far too wise for his age. Because God so loved the world that He gave His only begotten Son to live in and be of the world, we know that this Holy Babe must have cried like all other infants. Babies cry from their own discomfort. They are wet, or hungry or frightened or bored or discontented or cold or hot. They want; therefore, they cry.

While neither the scriptures nor the artists depict a crying baby, at least a couple of lyricists have heard that cry. A poem by Josiah Gilbert Holland became the lyrics for "There's a Song in the Air." Remember? "There's a song in the air! There's a star in the sky! There's a mother's deep prayer and a baby's low cry!" And John Rutter's "Candlelight Carol" begins, "How do you capture the wind on the water? How do you count all the stars in the sky? How can you measure the love of a mother? Or how can you write down a baby's first cry?"

If we view Jesus only as divine, then he cannot cry as a baby. He must be perfect in every way. Yet if He truly be the Word made flesh, He cried as a infant. It is only human.

Later scripture tells us that as a man, truly divine, truly human, Jesus wept, not out of his own pain as a baby cries, but in the acquisition of the pain of others. Like the blank wall's absorbency of the reflected image of wreath and candle, Jesus assumes the heartache of others. With compassion, he healed the sick, fed the hungry, forgave the sinner. Moreover, by both His words and deeds, He showed us how to live a life, not free of pain, but with compassion for the pain of others. He answered the age-old question: we are our brother's keeper.

We love the Christmas story because a newborn always brings promise. But if we leave the divine Baby Jesus in the manger through the coming new year, we miss the powerful message of His life lived in the world as a human being. Christmas takes on new meaning when we respond not only to the Babe's low cry, but also to the tears of the Man weeping in anguish for the whole world. We keep Christmas in our hearts only when we reach out to others as we would for a crying baby.

May the blessings of this holy Season be reflected in our words and deeds during the new year. May they always reflect the love of God for all of His children.

Recipient

...they presented him gifts. Matthew 2:11.

IT WAS THE USUAL Christmas pageant full of children in makeshift costumes. The little shepherds were garbed in plaid bathrobes with towels draped over their heads and tied in place with one of Daddy's old ties. The young wise men wore dressier robes and cardboard crowns. The angelic cherubs sparkled in tinseled halos. And each came bearing gifts for the make-believe Christ Child, a doll baby wrapped in a blue blanket.

Unlike most pageants, which occur in churches across the country, this one went pretty smoothly. No one forgot his lines; no one stumbled on stage and only a few sang off key. Mamas and Daddies smiled at each other and nodded approvingly at their offspring. What better way to teach them about Christmas than to let them be a part of the Christmas story?

The recessional began – first the shepherds traipsed off, followed by the wise men, and finally the angels flapped their arms and pretended to fly away. All departed, empty handed. The curtain descended on Mary and Joseph and the Babe in the manger. The applause was loudly appreciative.

Chairs scraped against the hard flooring as the spectators began to rise and greet one another. But a hush fell over then as a voice, unmistakably that of the young Joseph, blared over the still-live microphone. "What do we do with the gifts?"

What DO we do with the gifts? What a question for Christmas. Gift giving is very much a part of the season. And while the Scriptures admonish that it is more blessed to give than to receive, there is an obligation, which comes with every gift, and there is an art in accepting gifts.

The material gifts we exchange with one another should be accepted graciously. The joy one receives in giving shouldn't be lessened by protests from the recipient. "You shouldn't have!" "It cost too much!" are poor responses. "Thank you" is much more in keeping with the spirit of the season.

But more importantly, what about the spiritual blessings, which pour forth at this time of the year? Do we take time to savor them? Do we appreciate them? Do we even see them?

Likewise what do we do with the gifts we receive year round? What do we do with our God-given talents? Each one comes with the responsibility to develop it. And if we don't, we lose it. It is a simple lesson the Giver gives, but an awesome one.

What do we do with the gifts?

Gifts

And when they were come into the house, they saw the young child with Mary his mother, and fell down, and worshipped him: and when they had opened their treasures, they presented unto him gifts; gold, and frankincense, and myrrh. Matthew 2:11

Tater Tots

Every man according as he purposeth in his heart, so let him give,
not grudgingly, or of necessity: for God loveth a cheerful giver.
II Corinthians 9:7.

JUST FIVE YEARS OLD, he looked up to his nine-year-old
cousin. The older youngster had taught him how to hold a bat,
how to explore the nearby woods, how to maneuver a wad of
gum in order to blow a bubble. In the preschooler's eyes, there
was no limit to the knowledge possessed by his cousin, his buddy.

In late November, the older boy, sorting through his belongings, tossed out those items he no longer needed or wanted. "It's
for Toys for Tots," he explained to his wide-eyed cousin. "There
are boys and girls who don't get much for Christmas. Someone
takes these toys, fixes them up and gives them to the kids who
won't have a very big Christmas otherwise."

The next day, the five-year-old's mother found him sitting in
front of his toy box, examining each item therein. Beside him sat
a box. "What's the box for?" she asked.

"It's for Tater Tots," he responded, not turning from the task
at hand.

"Tater Tots?" she questioned.

"Yes, for the kids who won't get much for Christmas."

"Oh," she acknowledged, grinning at his childish malapropism. "And what are you doing?"

"Finding toys for Tater Tots."

Smiling, she left him to his self-assigned chore. It was a good lesson he had learned from his cousin, one that makes a mother's heart flutter a bit.

But, she still had her lesson to learn.

Hours later, long after she had forgotten his intent, he interrupted her; his arms barely reached around his box. "I'm ready to go now," he announced.

"Go? Where?"

"To Tater Tots."

"So, you've filled your box. Will you let me see what you've decided to give away?"

"Yes, ma'am," he replied, setting his box on the floor for her to look.

She picked up a car. "Why, your uncle gave you this car on your first birthday. It's one of those special things you keep up on your shelf."

He nodded.

"And these are your Tinker Toys. You have so much fun building with them. I don't believe you've ever lost a piece. Even the box is in good shape."

Again, he nodded.

Item by item, she examined the toys. Item by item, she recalled the good times he had playing with them.

"Are you sure you want to give away your good toys?" she asked. "I know you have toys you don't play with any more."

He nodded, then answered her. "When you give somebody something, don't you give them something that's fun to play with; don't you give them something special? You don't give them broken things, do you?"

The mother closed the lid on the box and helped him carry it to the car. Carefully, he set his box down in the nearest Toys for Tots booth and ran to the car without ever looking back once. Climbing into the front seat, he hugged his mother's neck. "I feel good," he said.

"So do I," said his mother. "So do I."

Gifts

For God so loved the world that he gave...John 3:16.

For Christmas, I will give my child...
    A breakable toy – all painted bright,
    Wrapped in gaudy paper, tied with a big red bow.
    It won't even last until next Christmas.
For Christmas, I will give my child...
    A tree that reaches to the sky,
    Entwined with silver garland and twinkling with lights.
    And he will cry when the pine needles fall on the rug.
For Christmas, I will give my child...
    A feeling of eager anticipation,
    A building, growing sensation of excitement.
    Anticlimactic with the arrival of the Event.
For Christmas, I will give my child...
    A belief in Santa,
    That jolly soul, that giver of gifts.
    In my heart, I know he won't believe for long.
For Christmas, I will give my child...
    A day of baking cookies,

Warm fragrances will fill the air.
And he will decorate the pastries, the kitchen and himself.
For Christmas, I will give my child...
An afternoon of package wrapping fun,
The corners of the presents won't be neatly tucked, the bows
will be all crooked.
It will take me the rest of the evening to clean up the mess.
For Christmas, I will give my child...
An evening of caroling,
A few moments of singing to people rushing by.
And he will be chilled by the night air.
For Christmas, I will give my child...
A feeling of warmth within the family,
A visit to grandparents nearby.
And I will long to visit my own family far away.
For Christmas, I will give my child...
A big day starting when he awakes at 3 a.m.
A running from this toy to that one.
A full day – forty-eight hours long.
But for Christmas, will I give my child...
An opportunity to care for others,
To share with others,
To know that it is truly more blessed to give than to receive?
But for Christmas, will I give my child...
A chance to know that the day is not glittery for everyone,
That some people will spend the Holy day alone because they
have no one with whom to share the day, their lives,
That no one will even care unless he cares?
But for Christmas, will I give my child...
The peace that comes in keeping true the spirit of Christmas,
Not only once a year on December 25.
But every day, every hour?
But for Christmas, will I give my child...
The yearning to adore the Christ Child,

To celebrate fully His birthdate and His life,
To experience the blessings of His love?
I pray that I can give my child the true Christmas gift, so that in turn, he, too, will know the joy of giving.

A Holiday Happening
or Two

...whatsoever things are true, whatsoever things are honest, whatsoever things are just, whatsoever things are pure, whatsoever things are lovely, whatsoever things are of good report, if there be any virtue and if there be any praise, think on these things. Philippians 4:8.

WITH EACH HOLIDAY THERE happens those poignant events which make one stop to think. Of such are these:

...Midst new shiny toys everywhere and wrapping paper knee deep, a three-year-old was found in the corner stacking boxes. Excitedly, he announced, "My build me a mountain!"

...And one box was too heavy for him to lift. Investigation discovered the baby inside. She had crawled in and was having quite a time amid the tissue paper. Her smile upon being found was enough to reveal her pleasure.

...Then, there was the memorable black-haired, brown-eyed youngster at one of the elementary school parties. Upon opening his exchange gift, he found a brand new soap pad box.

Disappointment immediately registered in his dark eyes. His teacher gently urged him to open the box, "just to see what might be inside." Sure enough, there was a big package of chewing gum and a snowflake paperweight. The glee in his eyes was as vivid as the disappointment had been the moment before. He was delighted to shake the gift and watch the snow fall; it was as if he had never ever seen such a sight.

...Then it was all over in one fatal accident; he bumped it off his desk. The fluid and the snow seeped from the container onto the floor and tears slid down his cheeks. There were other moistened eyes which helplessly watched his joy shatter.

...Sometime between the decorating and the serving of the Christmas birthday cake, the three-year-old snatched the "B" from Birthday. On Christmas Day, when the cake was served, it read "Happy Irthday, Jesus." The spelling may be a little off, but Happy Irthday, Happy Earth Day" isn't really a bad idea.

...Returning from a spend-the-night occasion with a friend, a ten-year-old breathlessly exclaimed, "Boy, did we ever have fun. We worked all afternoon."

...One Sunday, during the holidays, a college student substituted as a teacher in an eighth grade Sunday school class. Applying techniques found effective on campus, he demanded the young teenagers to answer, "Who are you?" Herding the class into a corner, he commanded them to shut their eyes and to ask themselves, "Where are you?" One very down-to-earth teen revealed the generation gap when he later described his reaction. "Good grief, Charlie Brown, where was he? I was standing right there in a crowded corner, my eyes shut tight with a guy shouting at me!"

...And finally, a seven-year-old eagerly asked, "Do we give gifts on New Year's?" After Mother berated him for being greedy, he replied. "I don't want anything, but Daddy lost his pocket knife and I thought getting him a new one would make a good Happy New Year gift!"

Hurting

...It is more blessed to give than receive. Acts 20:35.

THE ELEMENTARY SCHOOL CHRISTMAS parties were over. There were plenty of gifts to go around. Extra gifts had been purchased so that no one – not even the one who forgot to bring an exchange present would be left out. No one would be hurt.

Besides the exchange gifts, there were favors from the teachers, from the room mothers and from Santa.

Excitement mounted in every room as paper was torn from items and almost made it into the trash cans. For the observer, the colors of paper and ribbons blended in with the sounds of last-day-of-school shrills. It was hard to separate sight from sound.

And there were cupcakes, cookies, candies, gum, soft drinks, punch, fruit juices by the ton, enough to churn many a stomach ache. The children clamored and ate and unwrapped presents and played games and sang songs and made merry. It was a sight to behold.

Somewhere along the way, the children gathered around the teacher, like they do the birthday child, at present opening time. "Open mine! Open mine! Open mine..." they shouted and shoved gifts galore into the teacher's lap.

For long minutes, the teacher opened the tributes, admired each one and thanked the giver. It was the best part of the party. The young givers liked the warm feeling building inside themselves. They couldn't explain it.

Near the end of the festivities, near the time to go home for the holidays, one lone little boy approached his teacher. He hung his head and whispered low. He fought back the tears. For, he was a big boy now; he mustn't give in to baby ways. As the teacher wrapped her arm around the child, he buried his head on her shoulder and sobbed, "I don't have a present for you."

She tried to comfort him by saying that his being a very good student in her class was the best present he could ever give. "The very best gift I can ever receive is watching you grow and learn and be the best person you can be," she whispered.

He tried to smile through his tears, but even with those special words, uttered just for him, he still hurt. For a child, it hurts not to receive when everyone else is getting presents. Oh, but the pain is far worse when he wants to give and has nothing to give.

Half a Bar

So faith, hope, love abide, these three; but the greatest of these is love. I Corinthians 13:13.

HE WAS SPECIAL, A mentor, a friend. After having served as principal at one school since its opening thirty years ago, he was leaving, retiring.

Everyone around the first grader seemed sad. She could feel it. But even after having spent every school day on the campus for almost a year, she still considered herself a newcomer. The older kids had been around for ages, at least two years or more. Many of her friends bragged about the fact that this man had been principal when their mamas and daddies attended school. She didn't share that heritage. Resolutely, she took a bite from the candy bar in her lunch.

During "his" week, students and teachers alike brought him gifts. Mothers baked cakes and pies, dug into the pantry to send picture-perfect jars of jellies and pickles, and bundled up the early harvest from the summer gardens. His desk was laden with goodies. Although some of the gifts vividly revealed the stress of a school bus ride, like the squashed-in pie, they were still gifts. She nibbled while she thought.

Although she hardly knew him, except that he smiled at her every time he passed her in the hall and called her by name, she wanted so much to be a part of what was going on. Only, she didn't have a gift to bring. She played with the candy wrapper while she thought.

It's always more gracious to give than to receive, except when you don't have anything to give. Then it hurts. Undaunted, she was determined to show her love to the man everyone else loved, too. She took another bite. It was inspiration.

At home, she gathered a big bouquet, well all right, a little bouquet of wildflowers, a bud from every plant she could find. She even picked a sweet smelling gardenia from the neighbor's bush for her handful of posies. And she tied them with a big bow. She just knew he would like her gift, colorful, fragrant, because he loved flowers. But was it enough, really, for someone so special? She sniffed the flowers as she thought. Then she remembered.

The next morning, she proudly presented her gift to the principal. He thanked her kindly as he, too, sniffed the blossoms. She beamed with his acceptance of her token, for tied into the bow was the other half of her candy bar.

It may be blessed to give, but to share is to love.

Portrait of a Giver

...But she of her want did cast in all that she had, even all her living.
Mark 12:44.

AGE HAS GRAYED HER hair, dimmed her sight, wrinkled her skin, rounded her shoulders, trembled her hand, made uneasy her step, shortened her breath, bent her body. She is old. She will tell you so.

But her spirit is strong, undaunted by time or illness. She lifts her head high – even though there is pain in the movement. Like Santa, her eyes twinkle. Her face laughs when she smiles. The burden of time, which weights her body, gives her a mystic beauty.

She reminisces often. Life has been hard; life has been good. She worked many a year raising another's children; she birthed none of her own. Her memories focus on the good.

However, she is discontent. Memories, even the good ones, are not enough. She yearns to do, to give, to be active once again. She pushes her body; it does not move willingly. She nudges it again and again.

Every act takes major effort. She starts; she pauses; she starts again. What she once could do quickly and deftly now requires conscious determination. She refuses to give up.

As she sees it, there is so little she can do for others now. She is unaware that just being herself blesses others. She is not content to let others do for her. Action for action, she reciprocates.

All day, working a bit, resting a bit, she creates in her tiny kitchen. Her hands ache as she shells and chops pecans. But she does it. Her legs swell as she stands to mix a batter. But she does it. Always working some, resting some.

Finally, late in the day, she takes from the oven a steaming dishpan-sized pastry ring topped with coconut, candied fruits, and nuts. A confectioner's treat, she learned to make when she was very young, long, long ago.

It is a delicacy to see and to taste, a gift to give away.

But oh, it is so much more! For in her giving, she gives herself, her all.

An Orange for Christmas

But the fruit of the Spirit is love, joy, peace, forbearance, kindness, goodness, faithfulness, gentleness and self-control. Against such things there is no law. Galatians 5:22-23 NIV.

AS A CHILD, I delighted in finding oranges in my Christmas stocking along with a variety of other goodies. Although my family was poor by today's standards, my memories of Christmas are filled with abundance. Always, every Christmas, I found delicious oranges in my stocking.

In the mid 20th century, oranges were an expensive rarity in areas where orange groves didn't abound. We knew oranges through canned and frozen orange juice and of course, oranges at Christmas. What a treat. An orange today, no matter how plentiful they are in Georgia, one state over from the multitude of Florida groves, prompts fond memories of those Christmases past for me.

In a 1938 *Reader's Digest* article that I chanced to read during the 2020 COVID-19 shelter-in-place, Charlie Chaplin tells of one Christmas while he, at age nine, was housed in a British workhouse. For weeks, he had dreamed of receiving an orange and several sweets on Christmas Day. His daydreams revolved around how to make the treats last for more than one day.

However, since he failed to make his bed on Christmas Eve, he received nothing on Christmas Day. That night, two of his young roommates each gave him a piece of candy. The famed silent film star recalls how he was able to make those two bits of sweets last a fortnight. And this year, we complained about grocery shelves barren of our favorite items.

According to legend, oranges gained their place in Christmas tradition from the tales of St. Nicholas tossing sacks of gold down chimneys for the dowries of poor young women. The gold always landed in their stockings hung by the fire to dry. Today, oranges placed in Christmas stockings represent the gold, the generosity, of the famed saint.

Another legend has also evolved. The tale is the same; but in Denmark, the recipient is a girl; in Britain, a boy. Again, an orphanage is the setting and the protagonist, either the boy or girl, has failed to please the headmaster. Therefore, they receive nothing, not even the precious orange, on Christmas Day.

Nighttime comes and as they cry themselves to sleep, each feels a soft touch on their shoulders and an object shoved into their hands. It is a strange looking orange - a peeled one made of nine segments.

Instead of saving, admiring, and cherishing their oranges until a later date, their roommates, in an orphanage where ten children sleep in one room, have eaten almost all their oranges, but each gives up a slice for their sad companion. What an example of the Christmas message of unselfish love.

As we attempt to recover from the hardships caused by the invisible coronavirus, what do we give out of unselfish love? Are we all about recouping our own losses? By nature, are we merely takers or can we be givers, too? Do we realize that the gifts of the spirit come entirely by reaching out to our families, our friends, our neighbors, the strangers?

Jesus speaks of fruits. Grapes, olives, dates, pomegranates and figs are specifically mentioned by name in the Bible. But, Jesus never mentions an orange in any of his parables or sermons. However, his faithful follower Paul, in writing to the Galatians, tells about the fruit God does give in abundance to those who believe. What great gifts they are - love, joy, peace, forbearance, kindness, goodness, faithfulness, gentleness and self-control, each of the nine designed to be shared like the bequeathed nine segments of a shared orange.

May the fruits of the spirit lift our own spirits this Christmas. May the blessings of Christmas make happy our new year.

Wildflower

And Jesus called a little child unto him, and set him in the midst of them. Matthew 18:2.

YESTERDAY, HE STOOPED TO pick small purple wildflowers growing low on the ground. A classmate taunted him, "Say, what cha doin' that for?"

Indifferent to the challenge, he continued to scoop tiny blossoms in his grubby hand. He was intent on his quest. On arriving home, he thrust the miniature nosegay toward his mother's face. "They're for you. I picked them myself."

As if she didn't know. But with the grace that comes from years of accepting such love tokens, Mother smiled and spoke a simple, sincere, "Thank you."

Leaning over, she kissed him gently on the forehead and as if to emphasize her appreciation, she put the flowers in a glass of water and set them beside the sink where she could see them often.

He smiled. A gift of love had been given, accepted and returned. It was a simple thing.

Today is Saturday. He pauses in his play to pluck the yellow wildflowers growing along side the road. They have no fragrance. He repeats yesterday's ritual. And these yellow blooms join the purple ones in the glass beside the kitchen sink. He smiles.

Tomorrow, he will discover the orange wildflower growing in the woods. And he will pick it, too. And he will present it to Mother. And it will go in the glass by the sink. And he will smile. For there is something about a wildflower which makes a little boy pick it; and there is something about having flower in hand which compels him to give it to Mother.

What causes this obsession with the wildflower? Perhaps, it is only the youngster's realization that here is a gift he can secure all by himself. No one has to take him to town to shop. No one has to tell him the item is too expensive to purchase and give. No one stands over his shoulder and criticizes his choices as inappropriate. From thought to deed, every action is his own.

But who can explain it fully? It is a phenomenon in its own right.

Just as surely as the camellia faded, the azalea and dogwood greeted spring and died, the daylily withstood the summer sun, so, too, the poinsettia's flame will soon be cultivated.

But as long as wildflowers bloom and as long as there are little boys to pick them, the two will attract one another to the exclusion of the formal floral elegance. And mothers will continue to keep glasses of water beside the kitchen sink to hold the posies they receive. To a child's unsophisticated eye, such beauty can't be beat.

In all its simplicity, it is a complex thing.

Receiving

To everything there is a season, and a time to every purpose under the heaven...A time to get and a time to lose... Ecclesiastes 3: 1,6.

A TONY AWARD RECIPIENT clutched his trophy and exclaimed jubilantly, "Sometimes, it's better to receive than to give!"

Recall the joy that comes from a sense of real accomplishment, whether or not it is marked with a visible sign like a trophy, and understand what this actor, who has just been voted "best," is saying.

But for all its implied selfishness, there are other times when it is far better to receive than give.

No, it's not at any of the numerous gift-giving occasions celebrated throughout the land – Christmas, birthday, graduation day, wedding, anniversary, Valentine's, Mother's Day, Father's Day.

Certainly, receiving presents, being remembered at these times, is pleasurable; and being forgotten hurts. But also, at these times, expectations so often fall short. How many children, surrounded by mountains of gifts on Christmas morn, feel let down and complain, "Is this all?"

More often than not, the real pleasure at these times, like the scriptures say, comes in the giving, in knowing that you have made a loved one happy.

But...

It was a surprise visit from someone who had never stopped by before. It was a short stay, to the point, not much small talk. There was a purpose in his coming.

Hesitantly, he extended a small, yellowed box housing a delicate bijou once worn by his beloved. Now, he wanted to share it with another as a way of expressing his gratitude for an ordinary, everyday act that had seemed extraordinary to him.

And hesitantly, the recipient accepted the gift, overwhelmed by both the unexpectedness and the gentleness in the offering.

"I had a hard time finding out who had been so kind to me," he explained. "There is no monetary value to this pin, just a little something she enjoyed wearing. I want you to have it...if you want it."

"Want it?" the recipient replied, tears stinging her eyes. "It's beautiful. I'll treasure it always. But, the thought is even more beautiful. Even though your wife is no longer with us, the love that you shared with each other for over fifty years still radiates to others. Friends and lovers, you two exemplified what married life is all about."

And the recipient was truly blessed.

First Bike

Learn to do well. Isaiah 2:17.

MORE OFTEN THAN NOT, we remember first things first. It's not that we regularly put most important things first. Rather, it's a matter of remembering the first time events – the first day of school, the first kiss, the first bicycle - a gift from Santa.

Today's children have more opportunity to learn to pedal their own vehicle than did yesterday's child. Besides the traditional tricycle for preschoolers, there is a variety of vehicles, sports cars, scooters, tractors, firetrucks, pickups, all propelled by foot mechanisms. And today, bicycles themselves, with training wheels, come in all sizes. Counting the increase in geared and motorized two-wheelers, we've come a long way from the once standardized 26-incher.

Even so, the joy of mastering the art of riding a bike, without any help, mechanical or human, is universal. In other words, it's great to learn to ride a bike all by yourself. And when he's only five and masters the 20-incher, he feels nine feet tall.

It's not easy, you know. First, he must muster up enough courage to try that new fangled creature which is missing those comfortable training wheels. There's an awful lot of "wait-a-minutes." But then, with teeth gritted together and an all-business attitude, he's outside, ready to go.

He's up and on it. He's ready to go. The force of the push takes him, maybe, three or four feet, and he's down with the bike on top of him. Up again and again and again. He refuses to cry, but the moisture from his eyes meets the dirt from the road to create a mudpie face.

Each try - you've lost count of the number by now - seems to mean that he's losing ground. You want to take him in your arms and comfort. "It doesn't matter. You can try again tomorrow." But his determination keeps you away. You grimace with yet another fall.

But if you marvel at his determination, you are amazed at older brother's kindly patience. This larger child requested the task of teaching his younger brother. He's equally determined to master the art of the instructor. Enlisting the aid of a friend, he picks up the bike again and again and starts his young pupil all over. What's even more unusual, this older child, who is usually so loud and boisterous, keeps his voice low. Not once does he yell with impatience. You are witnessing yet another facet of each child.

In less than an hour, an eternity to those of us watching the drama, the five-year-old rides two feet – three feet – eight feet – twenty! He's done it! He's riding a bike! Again and again, from one end of that dusty road to the other, he keeps that bike upright. He's sitting tall; he's conquered it.

It's a magical moment when he's learned to balance the bike. And he's learned to travel in a relatively straight path. What makes it work? That is one mystery man has yet to explain.

He must still learn to get on and off the bike without so much difficulty. And he still must learn to manipulate corners better. And traffic rules. And safety. There is still very much to learn, but he can say with pride, "I can ride my bike!"

That night, after a warm bath, he eagerly snuggles down into the covers. He's a tired little boy. He wears all the bruises of the day like so many merit badges. Just before he closes his eyes, he whispers, "Bubba says that 'I can't' is a dirty word. Is it?"

Sage

A friend loveth at all times... Proverbs 17:17.

ONLY A HEDGEROW AND single car dirt drive separated Patsy's house from mine. We were inseparable. Or rather, I tagged doggedly after my neighbor.

Being three whole years older than I, Patsy was the brother and sister I didn't have, second mother, confidante, teacher, playmate. She was eleven, going on sixty-two, and didn't even know it.

Patsy created a secret place for us in the middle of the hedgerow. It only took a little molding to turn a natural opening into a green-walled cave. She swept the ground until it was hard and smooth and cool.

And hidden from the rest of the world, we whispered secrets, feasted on peanut butter and jelly sandwiches and felt safe. She never teased nor taunted nor tried to boss. And as the morning glories drooped their blue faces in the late afternoon sun, and the shadows stretched tall, Patsy's quiet presence flowered the air like lilacs do.

One Christmas, when I was eight, my folks splurged on a pair of silver-painted roller skates, the kind that clamped and strapped onto my heavy brown school oxfords and tightened with a key. I had wanted them for an eternity, at least a year.

"I'll teach you to skate," Patsy said.

And before the turkey was carved, we were out strapping on those metallic wings. And I fell down as soon as I stood up.

"Here, hold my hand," she commanded.

She guided me up and down the sidewalk. My skates scratched long, irregular gray lines on the concrete. As we reached the corner stop sign for the fifth time, Patsy said, "Okay, Kid, you're ready." And with that she turned loose of my hand and ran away.

I, clinging to that stop sign, screamed, "Patsy, come back! Don't leave me! Patsy! I can't skate. I can't!"

But Patsy didn't come back and none of the other neighbors so much as looked out the window at me. Finally, without an inkling that I could unstrap those uncontrollable wheels on my feet and walk home, I let go of the steadfast pole and fell down.

Again and again, I stood up, inched along a stretch of sidewalk between me and home and fell down. The rough concrete scratched my knees and elbows. Tears streamed down my dusty cheeks and stung the cut on my chin. "If I ever get home," I promised myself, "I'll never speak to that mean girl again, ever!"

When I reached home, Patsy was sitting on my front porch; her skates strapped to her feet. She smiled.

"I hate you!" I stammered. "You're mean." The sobs blurred the words, but the intent was clear.

Patsy grinned and spoke gently, as usual. "But, you know how to skate now."

She held out her hand. I wiped away my tears, took her hand and we skated around the block together.

Gifts that Keep on Giving

For God so loved the world, that he gave his only begotten Son, that whosoever believeth in him should not perish, but have everlasting life. John 3:16.

A GLASS HUMMINGBIRD FEEDER, topped with a red metal lid and attached to a red feeding base with six drinking holes, sways gently in the breeze. Suspended from a bracket attached to a back porch column, the feeder beckons hummingbirds during the spring and summer months. Once one of these small creatures sets up residence near the the feeder, he chases away all other would-be partakers.

When the sugar water runs low, the resident bird will fly close to anyone on the porch, then back to the feeder, then back to the person. Its message is as loud and clear as if the tiny feathered fowl could utter words. "Refill the tank!...please."

A dear friend, recently deceased, gave me this gift one Christmas years ago. At the time, four friends met monthly for dinner. It was a great chance for us to see one another, catch up on each other's news and just enjoy each other's company. We always had plenty of joint memories to share, too.

Shortly after we had established our routine, this friend suggested we exchange Christmas presents. She loved both giving and receiving tokens of love. Each year, she always found some novel gift for each of us. On occasion, she did not give us the same item; rather each was chosen for the individual in mind. When we exchanged gifts, she, almost childlike, could hardly wait until we opened hers. She so wanted each of us to be pleased. Pleasing us was far more important to her than any material item we could give her.

Shopping for friends, who were downsizing, was a more difficult task for me. I often settled for new Christmas tree ornaments or books, two of my favorite gifts to give and to receive. Always, my three friends received the same gift. But remembering my friend's enthusiasm perked up my shopping.

These days, two decades later, my husband and I still enjoy this hummingbird feeder. As much as it has been cleaned, filled and used, we marvel that it still is in good condition. Of course, hummingbirds don't weigh much and haven't abused the feeder.

And so one morning this past summer as I watched the humming bird drink his fill, I concluded that all gifts should bring as much pleasure as this one has given us.

I wish I could tell my friend how I feel. Since I can't, I opt to share my musings here. She not only gave her friends gifts; but for 19 years, she also directed the church's children's choirs which annually presented a traditional Christmas pageant in story and song - a gift for both the children and the audience alike, a gift that still prompts fond memories for me, and I hope, others.

And so, picture three young boys, clad in bathrobes with cardboard crowns painted gold atop their heads. Each carries a gift - gold, symbolizing kingship; frankincense, a perfume representing the priestly role; and myrrh, foreshadowing of death. As they walk down the aisle toward the stage, these pint size wise men sing, "We Three Kings of Orient Are."

One by one, they place their gifts beside the manger. And all the children in the choir, some dressed as angels, two as Mary and Joseph, others as the shepherds sing, "Away in a Manger."

Can you hear those youthful voices a-caroling? And the director, in a lullaby, then lifts her voice to sing, "Sweet Little Jesus Boy."

And what did the real Mary and Joseph do with those expensive gifts similar to the ones often presented to secular kings of the times? According to most Biblical experts, they sold them to finance their escape from King Herod. These gifts, memorialized in scripture, served the purpose of a gift given freely, and received humbly and gratefully.

A hummingbird feeder, a gift that keeps on giving, sways gently in the breeze to remind me not only of my friend and her giving ways, but also of all of the gifts from God, the Creator. This month we celebrate the birth of His Son, His most precious gift.

May all gifts that we give this season keep on giving pleasure for years to come if only in memories.

Show and Tell

For this is good and acceptable in the sight of God our Savior.
I Timothy 2:3.

THE MOTHER BROUGHT HER shoe to class. Of course, she wore shoes on her feet, but she brought her special shoe to her college English class for show and tell. To encourage these freshmen to utilize details in their writing, the innovative instructor had turned to the ever popular elementary school method of show and tell. The mother brought her shoe.

Before she ever displayed her shoe, she told her story. Earlier in the week, she had been ill, so very ill that all she wanted to do was lie quietly on the couch. But, her five-year-old daughter was so attentive to the woman. The child, by frequently awakening the mother from a drowsy sleep, kept checking on her condition. "Are you feeling better?" the youngster would ask. The mother kept hoping the child would find something to amuse herself. She did.

After shaking the mother for the umteenth time to see if she were feeling any better, the little girl asked, "What are your favorite shoes?" Mother's antenna should have gone up, but the woman felt too sick to respond appropriately. After much prodding, the mother finally whispered "My blue ones."

Then all was quiet. The mother drifted off to sleep. The child stayed busy for over an hour. Then she was back at the couch. "Wake up, Mama." The little girl shook her mother again. "This will make you feel all better." There, the child stood, a big smile on her face, loving concern in her eyes, and a once ivory-colored high heel shoe in her hand.

Only the shoe was no longer neutral in color. Painstakingly, the little girl, armed only with crayons, had created a rather uniformed patchwork design over the entire footwear. The toe was blue; the heel green. In between, pink and orange and purple squares covered the entire surface. "Isn't it pretty, Mama? I colored all the colors to make you feel better."

The mother sat up and took the shoe. Suddenly, her sick headache was gone and a new one had taken its place. How to respond? With her head pounding, the mother quickly weighed the joy in the child's eyes versus the cost of a pair of new shoes. The mother made the right choice. She hugged and thanked her little girl for wanting to help her feel better. She bragged on the child's ingenuity and propensity for colors and patterns. They studied the shoe together and admired the artwork and the love. The mother kissed the child and put aside the discussion about destruction of other people's property until later.

"Tomorrow," the child said as the mother tucked her into bed. "I'll color the other shoe just like this one so you can wear them to church on Sunday."

As I listened to the story and tears glistened in my eyes, so many thoughts crossed my mind. How many times do we adults hurt one another out of our own good intentions? Like the little girl, what we think is best for someone may not really meet his needs. How often do we say something painful to others and rationalize, "It's for your own good."

In studying the shoe, I questioned once again what do we adults do to the creative powers that lie within each individual between the ages of five and fifteen? How I would like for my teenage students to dig deep within for that spirit which picks up a variety of colors to paint, figuratively, pictures with words like the little girl colored the shoe.

And I was grateful that the mother brought her shoe for show and tell. How proud her daughter, a pro at the weekly kindergarten show and tell, must have been. Out of love and concern for the most important person in her life, the child had given a gift and it had been unconditionally accepted and used. It is the manner in which all gifts should be accepted because it is the way we learn both to give and to receive.

Time and time again, we hear adults admit how hurt they were as children when their parents, the no-frill ones, would exchange a gift chosen for them for something more practical. When we reject a child's gift, the child sees it as rejection of himself. How graciously we learn to accept gifts is far more important than whatever the gift may be.

As we enter this holiday gift-giving season, we are constantly reminded that it is more blessed to give than to receive. It is. But it is equally important to accept gifts offered in love with love. For by our very actions, we, too, give.

Polishing the Stone

Arise, shine; for thy light is come and the glory of the Lord is risen upon thee. Isaiah 60:1.

LIKE A MAGNET, ROCKS reached out and grabbed the youngster when he was in elementary school. He didn't skip rocks nor throw them, but he always had two or three pebbles in his pocket. "They just jumped in there," he explained. He kept rocks on his dresser like other people save pennies.

For a social studies fair project, he prepared a presentation on mankind's use of rocks over the years. He collected an assortment of tomahawks, other weapons, tools, fire-making flint. He even built a miniature dam of rocks.

However, rock polishing took center stage. Once on vacation, his family had stopped at a tourist trap rock shop, and from then on, he was hooked on the hobby.

Needless to say, Santa brought him a rock polisher that year. His parents read the directions because in his eagerness, he just wanted to throw a few rocks into the machine and turn it on. It didn't take long that Christmas night for the apparatus to be banished to the garage. Rock polishing is a noisy hobby.

Every day, he would run to the garage to see if the tumbler still was spinning. "Is it time, yet?" he asked. A perpetual motion machine himself, he wasn't mesmerized by the constant spinning and humming. A quick check and he was onto something more active. The slow process of allowing grit, water and motion to grind a plain piece of rock into a smooth shiny stone bored him. Magic, to him, supposedly occurred instantaneously.

Finally opening day arrived. As the rocks tumbled onto the table, even he acknowledged that the results were worth the waiting. He picked each one up and rubbed the slippery surface, not a rough edge anywhere. He marveled over the beauty of mottled color. Immediately by gluing a polished rock into a cheap setting, he began making jewelry for every member of the family. They received everything from earrings to bracelets, tie tacks to key rings. The heavy stones soon broke their bind to the metal, but his mother still has a piece or two tucked away in a drawer.

When he finally outgrew his hobby, his young cousin inherited the machine. Likewise, her noisy hobby was confined to the garage. However not long ago, the boy, now grown, asked the whereabouts of his rock polisher. He was a bit wistful that his parents hadn't kept it around.

*****

A musician talked about another kind of rock polishing on a television show. This octogenarian immigrated with her family from Switzerland when she was still a child. They settled in the Northeast where she continued her music lessons. Once grown and married, she and her husband financed the establishment of a music department at a small college. Quietly over the years, she taught music, performed, and organized musical programs for the community. Only of late has the music world recognized her talents as a pianist, singer and conductor.

"They call you a jewel among musicians," the television commentator said.

With the wisdom and modesty of one content with her life, this spry woman with gray hair, cropped short, laughed. "Me, a jewel? If I am a jewel, I am just one among thousands. Everyone has a jewel within. It is our responsibility to polish it until it shines."

The program focused not on her talent, but rather her use of that talent. Years of practice fine tuned her skills, but her greatest accomplishment lay in the numbers of people whose lives had been enriched through her music over and over. Through good and bad, like a rock tumbler spinning endlessly, she entertained with her talent, instructed students, introduced the novice to the world of beautiful sound. And then, they crowned her a jewel.

She gently protested, claiming within everyone lies the potential to be a jewel, to influence lives positively. It's not a romantic notion, but rather a charge to endure the grit and grind in order to perfect a God-given talent. She made me want to crank up my own sluggish internal rock polisher. However, most of us, like the young rock collector, grow impatient with the wait and struggle. It is easier to settle for rough rocks than to labor at polishing the jewels. Yet when we look for sheen in the shortcut, we are disappointed because it's not bright. But only we can polish the gem within.

Jingle the Joy Bells

Praise ye the Lord. Praise God in his sanctuary: praise him in the firmament of his power. Praise him for his mighty acts: praise him according to his excellent greatness. Praise him with the sound of the trumpet: praise him with the psaltery and harp. Praise him with the timbrel and dance: praise him with stringed instruments and organs. Praise him upon the loud cymbals: praise him upon the high sounding cymbals. Let every thing that hath breath praise the Lord. Praise ye the Lord. Psalms 150:1-6.

SNOW COVERED THE GROUND as the young family hurried toward the church for a Christmas Eve Vigil. The babe in the mother's arms slept soundly, but the preschooler, dressed in bright red footed pjs made of blankety material, squirmed in Dad's arms to be put down. She shook her dark curls with the anticipation even she, at such a young age, could sense.

At the entrance, ushers handed each child a bell. Her blue eyes widened with the gift. Holding it by the handle, she shook the small golden bell gently, and it rang. She grinned and shook it again. The family took end seats in one of the pews encircling the altar of a contemporary sanctuary constructed of neutral woods and glass. The priest invited the children to ring their joy bells with each musical selection. There was a lot of music that night and even more joyous bell ringing.

This child was fascinated when the singers, each carrying his own microphone, walked in procession down the aisle. After the choir had passed, she, with bell in hand, slid from her dad's lap and stepped into the aisle. And with each musical selection - and there were many - she not only rang her bell with all the other children in the congregation, she danced. She rang and danced. And while baby brother slept the night away in Mom's arms, sleep eluded her...but Christmas came.

Christmas Day, she taught her little brother how to ring his bell. It didn't take him long to learn, and together, they made the whole house jingle with joyous noise.

From time to time, she will take her bell down from the shelf where it is displayed. It always makes her smile. Holding it with reverence, she'll ring it, softly at first, then with great joy. And she begins to dance. For her, the joy that is Christmas comes all year.

The bell, a simple sound-making device, a percussion instrument, dates back to all chief nations in antiquity. By the eighth century, however, the Christian church not only had taken another pagan object and made it holy; the bell had become an essential part of the church itself.

Because average folk had only the moving sun to indicate time, the church rang bells to summon worshippers to services. Bells also rang to announce death and evening curfew, notice to extinguish fires and lights and to exit town streets. "All's quiet, all's well."

Since then, church bells have become popular within church services themselves as handbell choirs ring out the anthems, at weddings where a pair of bells often symbolizes husband and wife, and with the advent of a new year and most especially at

Christmas time when bells ring out great joy. Bells and their cousins - carillons and chimes - ring, peal, knell and toll.

However, the joyous celebration of the Birth of Christ dates back even further, to the presence of the angels who brought good tidings of great joy to the shepherds watching in the field. And with the announcement, the angels proclaimed the underlying message of the Son of God - peace, good will to all mankind.

Do we hear the joyous bells that ring on Christmas Day? More importantly, do we, like the child, ring those Christmas bells with great joy? Do we heed their message?

Advent

Prepare ye the way of the Lord, make his paths straight.
Matthew 3:3

Dusting off Christmas

*And the shepherds returned, glorifying and praising God for all they
had heard and seen, as it had been told them. Luke 2:20.*

WEARY FROM THE FRANTIC, hectic, frenzied pace of get-
ting ready for Christmas,
    I finally dragged the box of tree decorations down from the
    attic.
    The dust made me sneeze.
    The family gathered around excitedly.
One more chore to do today – trim the tree.
    I ached with the prospect of bending and stretching –
    All to make a dead tree come alive with imitation pomp and
    fine glitter.
Opening the box, I sneezed again.
    The fine mist of attic dust had sifted through the lid,
    Settling over all the tree's annual finery.
    "Just to make it all the more difficult," I grumbled.
I pulled the tangled string of lights from the box.
    "Where's the star?" asked the youngest, plundering in the
    box.

Plugging the cord into the socket, I painstakingly checked each bulb.

I felt soot coat my fingers with each twist.

Standing precariously on the kitchen stool, I started the string of lights

Down its long journey circling the tree.

The needles pricked my fingers.

"Oh, how pretty!" the children whispered in awe.

I shook the garlands and smelled the flying dust.

Again and again, I walked around the tree,

Looping golden streamers over green branches.

And again, the children praised the beauty.

With care I removed each fragile ornament from its protected compartment.

I smiled as I dusted them one by one.

"This is the first ornament your dad and I bought after we married.

And this one, dear Mrs. Bryant made for the newlyweds."

Attaching tiny wire hangers, I handed the ornaments full of memories

To the children...

"This one for baby's first Christmas, that's mine, isn't it Mom?"

And the youngest topped the tree with his star.

The children hung ornaments on every bough.

They tossed tinfoil icicles in the air, hoping they would land on the tree.

Catching snowflakes couldn't be more fun.

I remember. For, I, too, once was a child.

I spread the hand-embroidered tree skirt around the stand.

Quickly, the children stacked the presents in place.

Grabbing the broom, I began to sweep up pine needles, lost icicles,

And the dust.

Staring at the panful of silver and green discards coated in that irritating dust,

    I thought again about the way the dust sifted its way into the box.

    And the memories came flooding back to turn chore into pleasure.

    And I wondered why we pack away Christmas each December 26.

I turned to study the strange sight of hauling tree into house,

    And loading it with shiny, glittering bits and pieces,

    The house lights dimmed, only variegated tree lights twinkled above the crèche.

Setting the dust pan aside, I knelt to touch the figurines of the holy family.

    Of those who followed the star and heard the angels sing. I felt at peace.

    "It is so beautiful, it makes you feel good," whispered a child. "I want to share it."

    "We can share the feeling at least," answered another.

Today, I dusted off Christmas ornaments and hung them up to view.

    Tonight, the children dusted off Christmas for me to see –

    The spirit of Christmas – of loving life enough to share it, like misty dust –

    Can sift its way throughout the year. We need not pack it away.

Diangles

Even a child is known by his doings, whether his work be pure, and whether it be right. Proverbs 20:11.

'TWAS THE WEEK BEFORE Christmas and all through the house, people rushed frantically in an attempt to ready all things which make Christmas nice. There was a tree to trim, a cake to bake, a card to mail, a package to wrap, a party to attend, a song to sing...

Caught like a leaf in a whirlwind of fervor around him was the youngest. He, too, wanted to trim the tree, wrap the package, sing the song. And more times than not, he was just in the way, under foot, too young to be of any real help.

"Not now!" they said.

"Some other time!" they offered.

"Later!" they responded.

"Go away, little boy!" they meant.

But with equal determination, he refused to be put off. He had to be a part. Something very strong within refused to accept "later" as the only answer. Instinctively, he knew that "doing" meant being at the center. Also, he knew that "doing" made the time between now and Santa's visit come much faster. With the wisdom of a wise man, he knew that preparing for Christmas is as much a part of Christmas as Christmas Day.

Equipped with paper, glue, crayons, shells, buttons, discarded detergent bottles, plastic lids, paper cups, orange juice cans, clothes pins, glitter, whatever he could scavenge, he repeated all the lessons he ever learned in kindergarten, Vacation Bible School and day camp. Painstakingly, he drew holiday pictures, made his own Christmas cards and constructed ornaments for the tree – angels, cats, Santas, stars and diangles.

Diangles, for the uniformed, are either diamond-like triangles or triangular diamonds sprinkled with glitter. Cut from construction paper and topped with a loop of cord for hanging, diangles dangle from the lower branches of the tree, over the crèche, the holy scene, where they belong.

Crudely homemade, diangles are not found on the trees pictured in magazines. Nor are they found on trees decorated according to theme. Nor can you buy them in a Christmas store.

But as for me and mine, give us a diangle-trimmed tree any time. For diangles, made in love and without any expectations of gift in return, speak the message of Christmas.

Sounds of Christmas

He said, Yea rather, blessed are they that hear the word of God and keep it. Luke 11:28.

HAVE YOU HEARD CHRISTMAS? It is a very audible holiday. There's a song in the air; sleigh bells ring; chestnuts crackle as they roast on an open fire; hark! the herald angels sing!
Did you hear the happy "ho, ho, ho" of the legendary Santa?
    ...the bubbly giggles of his faithful fans?
    ...the uncontrollable excitement of anxious anticipation?
    ...the "I can't wait any longer" choruses?
Did you hear the escalating clamor of busy shoppers?
    ...the "I want this! I want that! Please?"
    ...the clinking rings of coins in cash registers?
    ...the "Would he like this? Will this fit?" laments?
Did you hear the crinkling of wrapping paper?
    ...the hustle to get packages in the mail on time?
    ...the whispered secrets in finding just the right hiding place?
    ...the shaking and rattling of each package under the tree?
Did you hear the chopping down of the traditional tree?
    ...the fragile jingle of ornaments being unwrapped?

...the "let me help, too!" whines of the youngest?

...the treetop angel sing?

Did you hear the clatter of pots and pans in the kitchen?

...the chopping and dicing and cutting and baking of tasty morsels?

...the bragging and boasting of each creative decorator?

...the closing of the lid on a full cookie jar?

Did you hear the cordial greeting of friends?

...even those who sent messages by mail?

...the warm responses of a family gathering together?

...the welcoming of family and friends with holiday cheer?

Did you hear the church bells ring?

...the lovely notes that the cantata sings?

...the amateur productions of the manger scene?

...the angelic voices with which the youngest worshippers carol?

Did you hear the whimper of those who hunger?

...the wailing of those who thirst?

...the sigh of a stranger?

...the groan of the naked?

Did you hear the moan of the sick?

...the lament of those in prison?

...the murmur of the lonely?

...the weeping of the unloved?

Did you hear the life cry of the newborn Babe?

Did you hear Christmas?

Did you listen?

Sing with the Christmas Cardinal

The birds of the air nest by the waters; they sing among the branches. Psalm 104:12.

ONE DREARY DECEMBER DAY in the mid-20th century, four-year-old Jimmy was determined to drive his trucks and cars around his mother's feet as she ironed the family's ever growing pile of line-dried, sprinkled cotton clothes. She kept telling her son to move before they both were burned. He'd move across the room but before long, his imaginary roads, or a little boy's need to be close to his mother, would once again lead to her feet. In desperation, she told him to be a good boy or Santa would bring him switches instead of toys.

"How does Santa know if I'm a good boy or bad boy?" he asked.

"A little bird will tell him," his mother replied.

As the child responded, "I don't believe that," he looked up to see a red bird perch on the outside window sill of their Dallas, Texas, home and peer inside. Jimmy believed.

Two years later, his mother died. But Jimmy continued to believe his mother's words. And that scarlet red bird became a familiar symbol of belief in things unseen in our extended family.

Across America, the cardinal is the Christmas bird adorning trees, cards, dishes, and napkins. Native to more than half of United States, it does not migrate. Therefore on the Eastern side of the country, it is not unusual to see a cardinal in winter. At least seven states claim this brightly feathered creature as their state bird and Fanny Flagg's *A Redbird Christmas*, set in Lost River, Alabama (2005), captures the feeling overtaking folks when they see such fiery plumage on a cold winter's day.

Because the male's color is such a bright red against the snow of northern states or even on a gray day in the South, it has become one of our country's contributions to the many legends surrounding Christmas. The legend of the poinsettia originated in Mexico; the Christmas tree, Germany; and the partridge, England. Santa Claus is an Americanized version of early Christiandom's St. Nicholas who sold his belongings to give to the poor throughout the land now called Turkey.

Jimmy's mother was right. In her essay, "Nestled in the Christmas Tree," Linda E. Allen writes that watch birds and the songbirds, including the cardinal, report to Santa about the behavior of all children. According to legend, watch birds can be seen perched on Santa's shoulder as they whisper in his ear the names of all good children. These birds are the red-suited man's "extra eyes."

The cardinal's color represents the love of the season. On his wings, he carries glad tidings of Christmas wishes and blessings of health and happiness for the new year. A glimpse of this red against the snow or on a wintery day, brings cheer, hope, inspiration; spring is not far away. But the legend begins before his assignment to Santa as a messenger.

Some 2,000 years ago, the cardinal joined the flock of birds gathered in a stable to sing for the Christ Child. When he flew away, his feathers took on the red color of blood that Christ would shed for the redemption of mankind. And once again as with legend after Christmas legend, God interjects himself into the secular and lays claim to all His creation. God does not distance himself from us; He sent His son to earth to show us the way. Rather, we humans try to hide from Him; but as Brother Lawrence says, "He is nearer to us than we are aware of."

According to the Rev. Matthew Henry, an ordained Presbyterian minister in 17th century England, best known for *Matthew Henry's Commentary on the Whole Bible*, birds sing throughout the Bible. About Psalm 104, he writes, "When we reflect upon the provision made for all creatures, we should also notice the natural worship they render to God. Yet, man, forgetful, ungrateful man, enjoys the largest measure of his Creator's kindness, the earth, varying in different lands. Nor let us forget spiritual blessings: the fruitfulness of the church through grace, the bread of everlasting life, the cup of salvation, and the oil of gladness. Does God provide for the inferior creatures, and will he not be a refuge to his people?"

And so for Christmas, we once again decorate our homes with scarlet plumaged cardinals. However, this bright red Christmas symbol is far more than a pretty ornament. It is a vivid reminder of the reason for the season - God's creation of all living things, God's love in a manger at Christmas, God's sacrifice on the cross, God's redemption on Easter, and our need to raise our voices, like the singing birds of the Bible, in praise and thanksgiving. When little Jimmy saw the red bird, he believed. The many images of cardinals surrounding us at this holy season offer us the same invitation to believe and to be grateful for that ability to believe in the unseen.

Anticipation

Wait on the Lord... Psalms 27:14.

IT HAS BEEN SAID that anticipation is half the fun of any event.

Anticipation is...

the countdown – 59, 58, 57 – of the last seconds before the start of the New Year.

the initial entry on page 1, January 1, in a new diary.

A young tyke commenting, with bewilderment, "I stayed up to midnight...once."

Anticipation is...

sighting the first display of Valentine cards,

sorting out just the right penny card from a package of one hundred for just the right person.

Hoping that someone special spends as much time sorting his cards.

Anticipation is...

noticing the first new green leaf of spring.

spying the first star at night.

Picking the first blooming daffodil.

Anticipation is...
    counting the days – 30, 29, 28 – before the birthday.
    sending invitations to a party.
    being.
Anticipation is...
    being aware that the swimming pool opens the first day of
    next week.
    being cognizant the school year ends a week later.
    being fitted for cap and gown.
Anticipation is...
    seeing red, white and blue everywhere.
    searching for the true celebration.
    wondering why July 4, 1976, falls on a Sunday.
Anticipation is...
    detecting the first crispness in the air.
    knowing the date of the first football game.
    refurbishing the fall wardrobe.
Anticipation is...
    making a whirl of parties and many plans before saying "I do."
    enduring the last, long, heavy days before due date.
    awaiting the visit of a grandchild.
Anticipation is...
    seeing Santa in the store windows before Thanksgiving.
    thumbing through the toy catalogue.
    having a part in the church's nativity scene.
Anticipation is...
    counting down the days on an Advent calendar – 12, 11, 10...
    being lifted up to place the star on top of the tree.
    trying to sleep on Christmas Eve.
Anticipation is...
    participating in the Hanging of the Greens.
    lighting Advent candles.
    attending Christmas Eve services.
Anticipation is...

knowing the Christmas story by heart.

realizing that the Christmas message lasts longer than the presents.

keeping Christmas all year long.

Anticipation is...

kneeling.

giving.

living.

It has been said that the let down feelings of the holidays come partly because reality can never match anticipation. But Advent, the anticipation of the birth of the Christ Child, is so much more than getting presents, wrapping up in warm feelings and toasting the New Year. Advent means waiting on the Lord, both with patience and in service.

Loneliness

Verily, I say unto you, Inasmuch as ye have done it unto one of the least of these my brethren, ye have done it unto me. Matthew 25:40.

LONELINESS IS A SENSATION that has pricked everyone's being at one time or another. For those already caught in the Christmas hustle and bustle, a little time spent alone is a pleasurable thing. But there is a vast difference in the pangs of loneliness and the precious moments of solitude. One is a burden; the other a blessing.

But experiencing loneliness sharpens our awareness of and concern for those who live with loneliness day in, day out. And without having endured loneliness, we could never savor so appreciatively the company of others; or for that matter, of ourselves.

...Loneliness is the sound of a bell in an empty schoolhouse,
    or a child lost in a crowd of adults,
      or the stranger, understanding nothing, stranded in a foreign land.

...Loneliness is the melancholy that slips in quietly on a Sunday afternoon, or a wave of homesickness,

or a hidden desire to be a child again – just for a moment and hear Mother comfort, "It will be all right."

...Loneliness is carrying any load, all alone,

or waiting long hours in a hospital for a loved one to recuperate,

or just waiting.

...Loneliness is the first star visible at night,

or the first jonquil to bloom,

or the last leaf on a tree.

...Loneliness is having to make a decision; and amid all the advice, knowing that no one can make it for you,

or searching for something to do to keep busy,

or having work to do when everyone else wants to play.

...Loneliness is having to stay inside,

or having to stay outside,

or just not being free to come and go as one pleases.

...Loneliness is thinking that no one understands your sorrow,

or thinking that no one else ever has experienced the depths of being so lonely,

or thinking that there's not a soul to call just to chat.

...Loneliness is the gnawing absence of peace,

or missing the fireworks,

or being awake, in bed alone, when the New Year comes in.

...Loneliness is keeping Christmas all alone,

or not having anyone who even cares whether you do or not,

or not even caring about anyone else.

Thanks

It is a good thing to give thanks...Psalm 92:1.

"IT IS MORE BLESSED to give than to receive." And it is. There is unequaled joy in giving a loved one the pleasure of a gift long yearned for. Excitement of anticipation runs high as the giver plans, selects and presents his gift.

How often the best thanks, the only thanks, is the look of ecstasy on the face of the recipient. One Christmas, a young husband bought a clothes dryer for his even younger wife – a most practical gift for a family with a baby. She was very appreciative, especially of the thoughtfulness that prompted the gift, but her pleasure in receiving could never match his in giving.

He spent at least a week in planning his strategy to keep the oversized gift a surprise until Christmas morning. He arranged to have it delivered to a neighbor's house late Christmas Eve. He coerced another neighbor into getting his wife out of the house at the appropriate time, a most difficult task since she had worked all day, was tired, and did not want to leave home for any reason. And he asked yet a third neighbor to help him move the dryer from its hiding place into his house. All of this contriving added to the surprise of the gift itself.

And to give to someone in need, to give anonymously to meet both need and human dignity brings private joy, secret joy, deliciously savored all alone.

Yet, there is a real art in being able to accept graciously, in being able to say, without protest, thank you. We all know those people for whom no one can do because they are always repaying by doing twice as much in return. It is almost as if they feared indebtedness. It is a gift in return to be able to say sincerely, "thank you," and not, "Oh, you shouldn't have!" How often has a recipient destroyed the pleasure of giving a carefully selected gift by returning it the next day.

Recall O'Henry's classic tale, "The Gift of the Magi." The young hero sells his heirloom watch to buy his wife a jeweled comb for her long hair and at the same time, she sells her hair to buy him a watch chain. The story, of course, illustrates the great gift of sacrificial love. But there wouldn't have been a story; it would have been all for naught, if either had refused the other's gift on the grounds of impracticality.

In America, in both the secular world of store decorations and in the spiritual one of Advent, the celebration of Christmas begins at the national holiday of Thanksgiving. We complain it comes too early, but perhaps it is fitting that we should start the gift giving season by first giving thanks.

Thanksgiving is a traditional acknowledgement of the year's blessings. Do we accept these many gifts, our blessings, without protest, but with a simple, sincere "thank you?" Do our faces reveal the ecstasy of receiving much. Saying thank you, without protest, for the year, for life, for a bountiful harvest, gives praise to the Giver. It is good to give thanks.

Good Cooker

In everything give thanks... I Thessalonians 5:18.

"HAPPY BIRTHDAY TO THE best cooker in the world!" the ecstatic child said as he hugged his mother's neck tightly. In his eyes, his birthday party was a success, the best ever.

His joy came forth in a childish turn of words, but his message was very mature. At that moment, Happy Birthday was the best feeling going; and his mother, the baker of a chocolate birthday cake bright with candles, was, in part, responsible for his good feelings. He wanted to reciprocate. It was a simple matter of saying, "Thank You."

Come Thanksgiving, we might pause – if we think of it – between football games and turkey wings, to give thanks to God for our bountiful blessings. Our ancestors stopped in the midst of eking out an existence to give thanks. But then maybe, when blessings are few, it's easier to recognize them for what they are.

However, like the birthday boy saw so clearly, there is a second aspect of giving thanks. For many of our blessings come at the hands of another. At one time, everyone of us has been helped by another soul. Did we stop to say so? The problem lies in the fact that we so often fail to recognize a gift; and if we do see it, we're too busy to stop to say "thank you." We're quick to fault, but for some reason, slow to thank.

Thanksgiving is the perfect beginning to the Christmas season. What better reminder of the spirit of the holy season is there than setting aside a day to give thanks not only to God, but also to His children?

Truly sincere, the birthday child passed along his marvelous, explosive feelings as surely as if he had gift-wrapped them and handed them to his mother. Strange, for the mother, too, the feeling was so warm and satisfying, multiplied by each remembrance of the moment, she wanted to pass it along to someone else.

"Thank-yous" work that way.

My Eyes Wake Up, Too!

Awake thou that sleepest...and Christ shall give thee light. Ephesians 5:14.

ON CHRISTMAS MORNING, THE two-year-old awakened at the usual hour. Instead of rushing her to the tree to see what Santa had brought, her parents sent her upstairs to see if the jolly, bearded man had come. While she was on her mission, they set up cameras. Dutifully, the child climbed the stairs and began her favorite game of hide and seek.

Grandmother soon joined the hunt for Santa. After they had checked all the closets in all the rooms, the woman asked the child, "Did you go to sleep last night? You know Santa won't come if you're awake."

Wide-eyed, the child explained. "I closed my eyes and went to sleep. When I woke up, my eyes woke up, too!"

Hand in hand, the two went down to see what Santa had brought.

Preschoolers always wake up their eyes. Of course, they don't see danger; we have to teach them that. But they can spy the tiniest object lying on the rug and pop it into their mouths if we don't watch out. Maybe that acute sense of sight explains their enjoyment for pictures hidden within pictures popular in children's magazines.

We adults also close our eyes when we sleep. Sometimes, we engage in this routine at inopportune times. If we're not embarrassed when we doze off in a meeting, church or the movies, our family certainly is. We sympathize with those who struggle to sleep, but for most of us, sleep comes easily.

And with the regularity of an alarm clock, we awaken in the mornings. At least, we climb out of bed. The trick comes in making sure our eyes and ears, our minds and hearts are also awakened.

Opening our eyes goes far beyond staying on task at work. When we really are awake, we look beyond ourselves. We become aware of our neighbor's need, of social injustices, of ways we can make a difference in the world.

Several years ago, people concerned about world hunger started a major campaign. Televised documentaries showed the massiveness of the problem, but the response was limited. The promoters were short sighted in their attempt to demonstrate the magnitude of the problem. First of all, people have a hard time watching mass suffering. They turn the dial instead. Secondly, when a problem appears beyond solution, people don't attempt to chisel away at it.

Today the same groups concerned about world hunger attack the issue in a different manner. Instead of depicting millions of starving children, they focus in on one.

When we look at any issue, one on one, we see ways to address it. When our eyes wake up, we begin to observe ways for taking problems apart in order to seek solutions.

If we truly wake up our eyes, then we see the positive and the good. It is so easy to focus on the negative and the bad. However, we all, children and adults alike, work harder, give more, do better, spurred on by a little praise than we ever do when we're cut down by a lot of criticism. With this self-realization, I don't know why we tend to see only faults and mistakes in others. Author Alex Haley advises, "Look for the good and praise it." When we follow his advice, train our eyes to search out the good and offer praise, rather than expect the bad and criticize it, goodness crops up all around us like a runaway bed of petunias.

Lawn the Mow

And the earth brought forth grass, and herb yielding seed after his kind, and the tree yielding fruit, whose seed was in itself, after his kind: and God saw that it was good. Genesis 1:12.

HE'S JUST A LITTLE tyke, only four. He has to look up to see three fourths of the world. He tiptoes to see more.

And, while he's always looking up to see the grownup world, he makes adults stand on their heads to see his. Why must one read from left to right to make sense of the words? It's just as easy to print right to left. Why can't cows be purple and jump over the moon? Why can't you lawn the mow?

Sure, for parents, mowing the lawn is work. And, too soon, that little tyke will grow up and learn that spending money can be made by mowing the lawn.

Even the words, "mow the lawn," sound harsh and commanding. Pick up the sticks and rocks to clean the yard of debris. Cut in even rows, back and forth, back and forth. Rake. Trim the flower beds. Edge the walks. Sweep. Clean. And when it rains a lot, repeat it all again next week.

And for those physically unable to tackle the job, it's a chore to find someone willing to spend the necessary time to manicure the yard just so. From start to finish, even atop a motorized riding-machine, it's work...anyway you look at it.

However, our little fellow's "lawn the mow" has a poetic cadence to the words. It brings a smile to the lips. The charm of youthful innocence is contagious.

For him, gathering rocks and sticks is just an out-of-season Easter egg hunt...made special because Daddy works by his side.

And if perchance, the grass cutter offers him a ride on the riding machine, it's magic. Hugging the driver tight, the miniature hitchhiker rides it like a magic carpet. First, he's the workman. But soon, he envisions himself riding a motorcycle, piloting a plane, manipulating a crane, sailing a ship to the stars.

Over the droning hum of engine, he tries to question the driver. Dissatisfied with the lack of answers, he settles down into a private silence. For him, the riding up and down the length of the yard ends much too soon.

"Why rake?" he asks, as he, now free of shoes and socks, scoots through the freshly cut blades. They stick to his feet. He likes the cool, wet feel of soft grass cuttings beneath his bare feet. Why rake up and discard such tickling pleasures, indeed?

He watches a bee dart in and out of an opening bud while his folks look down to trim the runners off evenly. For them, there's not time to appreciate the aesthetics.

"Work, work, work," he chants as he tries to imitate their actions. "Work, work, work," he continues as he retraces, now atop his tricycle, the paths made by the powerful, big, riding machine.

The well trimmed yard now harmonizes with the musical upside down phrase, "lawn the mow." Will his parents stop long enough to see the beauty of both? If so, then, why are they surprised the very next day he's ready to "lawn the mow," again?

Joyous anticipation adds to our worship during Advent while we await Christmas Day. Like the child understanding that the yard must be cleared of rocks and limbs before climbing aboard the exciting ride, it is a time for preparing our hearts, ridding them of stumbling blocks, to receive the Christ Child. Let us not burden ourselves with too many chores. And like the child eager to "lawn the mow," everyday, we should welcome with open arms this time of expectation. For what God has created, He deems good.

Asking for Seconds

Then came Peter to him, and said, Lord, how oft shall my brother sin against me, and I forgive him? Till seven times? Jesus saith until him, I say not unto thee, Until seven times: but until seventy times seven. Matthew 18:21-22.

FOR CHRISTMAS, THE THREE-YEAR-OLD has asked Santa for a second kitchen. Early on, this child became fascinated with cooking utensils. She soon graduated from her mother's pots and pans when she received her very own play kitchen. She's spent hours stirring up imaginary dishes.

However, when the family screened in the back porch and turned it into one of the favorite places for the family to gather, she made her request for a second kitchen. She had quickly become weary of hauling all of her kitchen paraphernalia from playroom to sunroom and back. Hopefully, the Easy Bake Oven she received for her December birthday will suffice for the time being.

As a friend considers remodeling her kitchen, she seeks a stove with two ovens. She says that she doesn't need that second oven every day, but when she has company, a second oven would certainly make entertaining friends and family much easier.

Our oldest grandchild, now in middle school, has two sets of school books, one of which she keeps at home. The PTO purchased the second set to eliminate the many health problems created by children lugging heavy bookbags. Teachers also love the concept because it also terminates those annoying excuses from students for not completing a homework assignment because they "forgot" to take their books home.

Since Thanksgiving, how many of us have complained about overindulgence because we have been tempted by second helpings? As a nation, we love to eat, and we love to complain. The holidays seem to give us plenty of opportunity to do both.

We're a nation who believes in seconds. In my lifetime, I've seen many families move from houses with one bath, one car and one telephone to homes with at least two, and often, more of each of these items.

But what about second chances? Oh, we want them for ourselves. We all make mistakes, and we want the chance to correct them. The world owes us that much.

However, when it comes our turn to forgive, it seems so much more difficult. The injustices, the abuses, the slights we have encountered loom large. We make tiny mistakes; the rest of the world transgresses big time.

Of course for self-preservation, we sometimes must walk away from a situation. It can be mentally and physically unhealthy not to do so. And setting out into the unknown is always frightening. Sometimes, we must stand and fight. We can do no other.

However in day-to-day life, we too often nurse a grudge until a small inconsideration by another transforms itself into a monster. Think about how often many of us are offended when someone does not agree with us. We pride ourselves on saying that we can see both sides of an issue; but more times than not, those two sides are limited to my side and the wrong side.

No matter how much a transgressor may try to apologize, we can cultivate our own sense of hurt until it reaches the height of Jack's beanstalk. By pouting or by spewing cruel words, we truly can make another person uncomfortable. But the very act of constantly reinforcing our own grievances hurts us far more than those we try to punish.

During Advent, we encounter many glad tidings and much good will. We hear it in song; we read it in story; we see it on film. The totally decorated scene can warm us inside. It truly is a time for second chances, not only for others, but also for ourselves. For, when we can put aside grievances, both real and imagined, when we give others and ourselves a second chance to do good, we discover that peace promised in Christmas.

Give Us this Day

Give us this day...Matthew 6:11.

Thanksgiving is...
    a day off from work,
    and from school,
    a mini-vacation.
But for many, Thanksgiving is...
    a workday like all others,
    or, a day with no work to be had,
    work. The defining difference.
Thanksgiving is...
    a day ablaze in autumn colors,
    rich in pumpkin oranges,
    and cranberry reds.
But for many, Thanksgiving is...
    a drab and dreary day,
    for the soul clouded,
    by mourning black and gray forecasts.
Thanksgiving is...
    a day spent hunting,

a day for enjoying
the great outdoors.
But for many, Thanksgiving is...
    another day to fear the guns,
    and the men who make war
    in foreign countries and on city streets.
Thanksgiving is...
    a historical holiday,
    commemorating both
    survival and cooperation.
But for many, Thanksgiving is...
    a day for here and now,
    never taking the time to learn about history
    nor from it.
Thanksgiving is...
    A day for feasting,
    for turkey and dressing,
    and all the trimmings.
But for many, Thanksgiving is...
    another day of hunger,
    another day of foraging for food,
    another day of going without.
Thanksgiving is...
    a day for the family to gather,
    for grandparents and grandchildren
    to celebrate the generations.
But for many, Thanksgiving is...
    a day of loneliness,
    another day of being ignored,
    another day of ignoring others.
Thanksgiving is...
    a day for counting blessings,
    for giving thanks, for showing appreciation
    to others and God.

But for many, Thanksgiving is...
    a day when no one can look
    beyond his own pain.
    gratitude is not a part of the vocabulary.
Thanksgiving is...
    a few days before the start of Advent,
    the perfect beginning of the Christmas season,
    a time to go to our knees.
But for many, Thanksgiving is...
    a hectic time of shopping,
    fighting for a parking space at the mall,
    resenting all the work to be done.
For all of us, however, Thanksgiving is...
    a day, 24 hours, minutes ticking by,
    when it is gone, it is gone forever,
    never to be reclaimed.
For us all, however, Thanksgiving is...
    a day of our own making,
    we choose how we squander or savor each second
    it is a treasure set before each of us.

Give us this day...Let us give thanks for each moment. Let us open our eyes that we may glimpse the truth of time before it is too late. Let us see how to use wisely this gift given freely to everyone, some more, some less. Counting blessings isn't enough. We must make them count.

Learning Christmas

Take my yoke upon you and learn of me; for I am gentle and lowly in heart and you will find rest for your souls. Matthew 11:29.

SHE IS THREE YEARS old, going on twenty-five. But after all, she has an older brother to learn from and a younger sister to teach.

And her assimilation of the world is fun, not only for her, but also for everyone else around her. This summer, after she explained the function of her mother's sewing machine to a guest, he innocently asked if she could use it. She nodded and he responded, "Good, I have clothes in the car that need mending." Everyone present laughed and then proceeded to carry on their adult conversation.

When they missed the child, Mother, wise in the ways of her daughter, decided to check on her. And where did she find the youngster? Outside, diligently trying to unlock the guest's car with her set of plastic play keys. She was going to "fix his pants just as he had asked."

Then before Thanksgiving, Grandmother asked the child what she would like most of all for Thanksgiving dinner. Once again, the child disappeared, only to reappear long minutes later with her request.

"Waffles," she whispered in her grandmother's ear.

"What's that, Honey?" Grandmother responded.

And in a loud voice, she repeated, "Waffles, I want waffles for Thanksgiving dinner."

Since Grandfather is world famous, or at least acclaimed by all in the family, for his waffles, waffles they had. They were probably the only family in America that served waffles with the traditional fare of turkey and dressing.

Then Christmas, with all its trappings, approached. She "oohed" and "aahed" over each light and ornament for no other Christmas measures up in awe and wonder like the one when we are three years old.

With hands by her side, she walked from room to room in her grandparents' well-decorated home. She studied the traditional tree with its breakable ornaments, the small imported crèche, the hand-crafted ceramic tree that glows and plays music, the porcelain angel figurines, the dishes full of Christmas candies, the collection of Christmas music boxes, the ornamental candles, the magnificent pots of poinsettias and the lit nativity scene in the front yard. No doubt about it, the life-size figures of Mary, Joseph and Baby Jesus were favorites.

But one decoration puzzled her. "That's Santa Claus," she said pointing to a statue of the jolly old man in red. "But who is that?" she asked, pointing to his companion.

"Why, that's Mrs. Claus!" Grandmother exclaimed. "That's Santa's wife and we call her Mrs. Claus, just like everyone calls your mother, Mrs. Moody."

Grandmother paused a minute for the child to comprehend the comparison. Then the woman asked, "And who am I?"

The child studied her grandmother's face while she pondered the question. And then, she responded, "You're Mrs. Grandmother."

And we all laughed at the childish reasoning, infinitely wise.

By the time she's four, she will have learned Grandmother's married name and a myriad of other facts. She'll know much more about the holiday season and all its marvelous traditions. She'll learn more songs to sing and will have a larger repertoire of poems to recite.

And so it is with Christmas. Like learning something new each time we reread a good book, we also learn more Christmas each time we celebrate it. In fact, the ability to keep on learning through life is one of God's blessings for us.

As young children we learn to anticipate because we remember the fun of the previous year. Older children learn the hard lessons that some of their wants might not be fulfilled. Teens begin to relish the time off from school, the socializing with friends that come with the holidays.

Young adults enjoy the season as they watch it through the eyes of their own children. And older adults, who have experienced many phases of Christmas, can still marvel that the holiday seems freshly new each year.

Despite all the hustle and bustle, the commercialism, the fear that we won't finish all of our chores by Christmas Eve, this holy day offers us a chance to explore in one more way the deeper meanings not only of the Christmas message, but also of other lessons both in the Bible and in life.

We learn mentally by repetition. Likewise, in hearing annually the Christmas lessons of "Fear not, I bring you good tidings of great joy. For unto you this day a Savior is born...And on earth, peace and good will to all men," we eventually take it to heart. And in the yearly echo of story and song, we always will discover new insight if we approach the time with the eagerness to learn of a three-year-old going on twenty-five.

What Child Is This?

For unto us a child is born, unto us a son is given; and the government shall be upon his shoulders; and his name shall be called Wonderful, Counselor, The mighty God, The everlasting Father, The Prince of Peace. Isaiah 9:6.

WITH EVERY NEW ENCOUNTER, the two-year-old inquires, "What's this?" For the past year, he's sought the identity of everything from apples to zebras. At the present, he's fascinated by cars and trucks. He drives little ones around the house. He rides foot-powered ones in the back yard.

In the real car, he's back to his old question, "What's this?" as he turns on the windshield wiper. "What's this?" as he hits the horn. "What's this?" as he jiggles the gear shift. He expects answers, too. He learned early on the simple words: key, light, wheel.

He would rather be allowed to stay in the car and play with the gadgets than almost any other activity. He has already locked himself in the car with the only available set of keys. After much frustration to get him to lift the lever on the lock, his mother called the police. He fluctuated from interest in what the policeman tried to do to free him to fear when the man in the uniform tried to talk to him. I don't know who anguished the most over the predicament in which the child found himself.

As long as an adult is outside to watch, he's still allowed "to drive" the stationary big car; however, without key in hand. He wants the key. The other day, he discovered the door handle, the one which operates without a key. With one mighty shove, he opened the door and fell out on his head. And yet, he still wants to play in the car.

If his interest in automobiles continues at the same pace it has over the past year, it won't be long before he's asking, "What's this?" as he points to the transmission. "What's this?" as he reaches for a spark plug. "What's this?" as he follows with his eyes and hands the many belts and hoses under a hood. He hasn't asked those kind of questions because he hasn't crawled under the car yet. Nor has he figured out how to open the hood yet. If he had, he would have pushed a stool close, climbed up and began to poke and pry.

As trying as his question of "What's this?" may be to his parents, in another couple of years, he'll change. Then like his older sister, he'll ask "Why?" He will have the vocabulary, but he will want to know why things work the way they do. He won't settle for one word answers then.

At this holiday season, we're much like this child. We stay busy asking ourselves the simple questions. "What should I buy cousin Joe?" "When can we decorate the tree?" "How many cookies should I bake?" "Do I like the red or green wrapping paper better?" "When am I going to find time to address all the cards?" "Whose party is tonight?" "What time does the cantata start?"

And while these endeavors keep us entertained for the moment, they do eventually lead us to ask the more important question of "Why?" If not, all the hustle and bustle of December is for naught. It merely tires us out, makes us cranky, and drives people from our presence.

But when we finally get around to asking the big question "Why?" then, we can place the trappings in proper perspective in our lives, just like we hang ornaments on the tree. One plastic ball doesn't decorate a six-foot tall tree, but when all the lights and star and angels and tinsel and garland have been hung, no matter how old we are, how many Christmases we've celebrated, we still marvel at the beauty of a Christmas tree.

Likewise, celebrating Christmas is bringing all that we are and all that we have to place at the feet of the Christ Child for Him to use to decorate His world. The Babe of Bethlehem, like the little boy who loves trucks will eventually do, grew up. He fulfilled Isaiah's prophesy to become Counselor, mighty God, everlasting Father, Prince of Peace. If He hadn't, we wouldn't celebrate Christmas year after year. Likewise, He expects us to grow up, too, to ask the big boy questions, to discover the meaning of Christmas beyond the glitter, to do His work in His world.

Whether we're a child learning about our world or an adult learning about our world, we must always move from the easy questions to the hard ones. But when we learn the answers, life takes on new meaning.

Umbrellas

And the rain descended and the floods came, and the winds blew and beat upon that house; and it fell not: for it was founded upon rock. Matthew 7:25.

IT WAS A GRAY and drizzly December day, not fit for duck nor man. Rather, it was the kind of dreary day that taunts people with thoughts of being curled up with a good book in front of an open fire. Still, I had to be about the day's business.

No sooner had I pulled out of my driveway when I spotted him skipping down the sidewalk in tune to the rain. With his curly red hair and bright yellow slicker, minus hat, he was a vision of color. And he whistled and sang at the top of his voice as he danced along. Gene Kelly, eat your heart out.

All of a first grader, well, maybe no more than a kindergartener, nothing could dampen his spirits as he sped toward the school house. After all, Christmas was coming. He challenged the squirrels hiding in their nests, and he waved at the passerby. I couldn't help but smile.

Stopping, I watched him from a distance for as long as I could see him. He kicked a rock, picked up a penny and stuck it in his pocket. Maybe it was a worm. He stomped in several mud puddles, turned his face skyward to feel the rain and once, he even shook all over like a freshly bathed dog. He laughed out loud with the act. And he even looked both ways before he crossed the street.

It was an ordinary day, not the last day of school before the Christmas holidays. Maybe it was his birthday, more than likely, not. He was just glad to be alive and even the rain didn't inconvenience him.

I shivered, pulled my coat tighter around me and hurried on my way. But the miniature bundle of sight and sound haunted my thoughts for several days. In that short walk from home to school, he displayed a zest for living, for being able to smell both the roses and the rain. There was something in his being that most of us covet, yet fail to imitate.

While he may have been more animated than most, children have a way of enjoying the moment. It's a gift a lot of us lose, like his hat, somewhere along the way.

I still didn't want to get out in the rain. I had "more important" things to do that day and rain-soaked hair wouldn't make my job any easier. But he did make me stop and remember. And all live-long, sloppy day, I looked and saw things worth seeing. Maybe they weren't as important as the squirrels, the puddles and the worms, but I glimpsed the world through the eyes of a child and it was wondrous.

Wonder of wonders, Christ came into the world as a child. And time after time, he invites us to see His kingdom as the children do. Isn't it time to throw away our umbrellas and marvel at the wondrous?

The Spirit of Townsend

For the Spirit searches all things, yea, the deep things of God. I Corinthians 2:10.

NESTLED IN THE PINEY woods of South Georgia is a small community of a few hundred people. In a visible prayer for peace during the Persian Gulf War, a few neighbors, along one street in Townsend, Georgia, decorated their front yards for Christmas. They wanted a very visible reminder of the Christmas Spirit for one of their own returning from war. A massive "Peace on Earth" sign dominated the landscape.

Over the years, the neighborhood decorations have grown until from a distance, the little town glows like a big city decked out in neon. On closer inspection, commercial signs don't blink in Townsend. Christmas ones do.

"Look, Granddaddy, there's Rudolph!" the three-year-old exclaimed. "And another one and another one. There's Santa, and another one and another one... There's a star and another one. There's Baby Jesus and another one..." And his younger brother, still a baby, oohed and aahed and tried to point to each one.

Over the years, more and more neighbors have joined in until the traveler coming from any direction sees first one house, then another, then a whole section lit up like one giant Christmas tree. All of them decorate every spot in their yards with both secular and religious messages, images and sounds. The dominant message this year is "Wise men still seek Him." Not to be outdone by the adults, three little girls stood near the road at one house, waved and wished every passerby, "Merry Christmas."

Some of the decorations are store bought. Many, however, are handmade, crafted in the backyard workshops. With every decoration either lighted or spotlighted, the whole trip is like driving through a celebration of lights.

If any one of these houses were sitting all alone, the casual passerby would think the great variety of displays in the yard, were "gaudy, tacky, in poor taste." Yet together, they create such a spectacular sight, the onlooker catches his breath and oohs and aahs with the youngest. Yet, one cannot view this massive light display without cynically commenting on the light bill. We can make such poor judgments about others when we don't know the facts.

According to one of the organizers, power bills do go up dramatically during the two-month display. But she went on to explain the displays have touched the lives of so many people who just happened to drive by or those who came by especially to see it, the expense has been worth it. From all reports, the Townsend lights truly have become a ministry.

She's right. If you haven't found the true spirit of Christmas yet, make the trip. As you drive slowly down the road and try to absorb all that your eyes see, you'll feel the warmth of the lights and you'll marvel that so many people spend so much time to decorate and patrol nightly, replacing bulbs, securing decorations, watching for potential fires. You cannot come away without having been touched by the unified effort of so many in such a small town. Even the most blasé of today's young have to realize that what they witness goes far beyond the magic they find in their video games. It's not virtual reality; it's real.

As the three-year-old who saw so many Rudolphs and sang about each one, settled down into bed that night, he said, just before he drifted off to sleep,

"Grandmother, it's been a really good day."

She nodded. "Yes, it has. Do you know why it has been such a good day?" Half asleep, he shrugged his shoulders. She said, "It's been a good day because you made it a good day. You made it a good day for yourself, for your granddaddy and for me."

"And for my little brother?"

"Yes, for your little brother, too."

"Did I make it good for anyone else?

"Yes. You made it good for everyone you smiled at or spoke to."

Eyes still closed, he smiled, turned over and went to sleep.

Good days and Christmas can be ours for the making. Just ask a three-year-old or the people of Townsend.

Epiphany

...One thing I know, that, whereas I was blind, now I see.
John 9:25

Light

I am the light of the world. John 8:12.

SUNLIGHT GLIMMERED THROUGH STAINED glass windows. Tiny white lights glistened in a stately tree. Tinseled bells glittered under incandescent light. Christmas was upon us.

From the rear of the sanctuary, two young acolytes, clad in red robes and white cottas, proceeded down the aisle. Well aware of his duty to carry the taper high, one marched piously. The second nervously watched his flickering flame. Sure enough, midway down the aisle, an unnoticeable breath of air snuffed out his small light. Wondering what to do, he bit his lip.

At the altar, the two met and in the fashion of soldiers crossing arms, the darkened taper was relit, and both turned to the task at hand.

The first acolyte lit his candle easily. The second, still wary from the first mishap, trembled as he touched flame to candle. Nothing. He tried again. And again. He glanced at the nearest door. Oh, to throw the whole thing on the floor and escape! He said nothing, but panic clouded his countenance.

The minister arose from his chair on the dais, and walked somberly to the child. Kneeling, his black robe billowing across the floor, he pulled loose the wick buried deep in the wax and smiled at the child when flame burst forth with the first touch of fire. The youngster scampered to his seat on the front row and tried, turtle-like, to scrunch his head into his shoulders.

The candle flame fluttered and moved as if possessing life. Traditionally, candlelight has come to symbolize Christ's words, "I am the light of the world." Regardless of the real properties of flashlights, spotlights, headlights, such motionless beams appear lifeless; and we cling to the symbol of a candle whose flame dances with movement. The message of the Christmas candle is unmistakable – Christ is the light of the world.

But He passed it on. "Ye are the light of the world. A city set on a hill cannot be hid. Neither do we light a candle and put it under a bushel but on a candlestick and it giveth light unto all that are in the house." Matthew 5:14-15.

Starlight brightened the stable where He was born. Candlelight still symbolizes His life. But His purpose is fulfilled when a friend shares his light with a friend, and a man reaches out to assist someone in need.

Blessed Is the Tree...

Blessed is the man...whose delight is in the law of the Lord...And he shall be like a tree planted by the rivers of water, that bringeth forth his fruit in his season; his leaf also shall not wither and whatsoever he doeth shall prosper. Psalms 1: 1-3.

OUTSIDE, WINTER RAGED ONE February day in Chicago. No longer were the snow remnants pristine, rather, shoveled out of the way, they resembled piles of dirty, dingy, once-white socks. The lingering gray days remained bone chilling cold.

Inside, the three-year-old sat on the floor with galoshes, heavy coat, mittens scattered around him. His mother coaxed him to stand and let her help him put on his outside clothes.

"Don't want to go," he pouted.

"You don't want to go?" His mother quizzed. "You love T-ball!"

The little boy sat his ground. "Don't want to go."

"Why not?" The mother took him in her arms. "The gym will be warm, and we'll take off your coat and boots as soon as we get in. You like to hit the ball and run the bases. You know you like playing with your friends."

His lower lip trembled and a tear ran down his cheek. He looked up at his mother. "But I like trees."

*****

So do I, Nephew, so do I.

For that reason I found the North Rim of Grand Canyon National Park so much more beautiful than the South Rim, which I acknowledge remains the most spectacular panorama I have ever seen. From the desert South, one can stand at the rim and look at the wide expanse of this wonder unimpeded.

To view the same rugged landscape from the less visited North Rim, which rises to 8,800 feet, one must first travel through mountain forests of blue spruce, Douglas fir, ponderosa pine and quaking aspens. Here, the tourist drives from one overlook to another, viewing each magnificent vista, always framed by towering mountain trees, from a different perspective. Occasionally, one might also glimpse deer, turkey, coyote and Kaibab squirrel, which having lived such an isolated life, differ from squirrels elsewhere. Although we drove from each vantage point to the next, we walked the Angel Point trail outside of the North Rim Grand Canyon Lodge. Along this narrow path, we saw a deer nibbling leaves and talked with a couple from London celebrating their 40th anniversary. They had married on Pearl Harbor Day. With this, their third trip to the Grand Canyon, they, too, prefer the North Rim.

It was at the North Rim dedication of Grand Canyon National Park that President Theodore Roosevelt said, "Leave it as it is. You cannot improve on it. The ages have been at work on it and man can only mar it. What you can do is keep it for your children, your children's children, and for all who come after you..."

*****

Many people like trees. For that very reason at this time of the year, some folks haul trees, usually of the mountain variety, inside and decorate them with lights, tinsel, and sparkly ornaments. Others drag their artificial versions out of the attic. However, real or fake, the Christmas tree has come to symbolize this holy season.

In Germany many years ago, a missionary, St. Boniface, urged newly baptized Christians to set aside their pagan rites around the oak and instead, decorate a fir, which had sprung up through the roots of the larger tree, with tributes to the Christ Child.

Martin Luther is credited with adding candles to the Christmas tree to represent the Light of the World. "O Tannebaum, how lovely are your branches...Your beauty green will teach me that hope and love will ever be the way to joy and peace for me."

As we admire these decorated trees, stack packages under them, sing songs around them, let us always remember that the Creator of little children, trees and great wonders of the earth brought His son, Jesus Christ, into the world to teach us how to live like "the tree planted by the rivers of water that brings forth its fruit..." It is not enough merely to exist nor to celebrate His birth; we must also live His message.

Christmas, with all its trappings, including the Christmas tree, warms our hearts for a month, and we like the glad tidings. However, we truly celebrate the birth of the Christ Child when our lives, like shiny ornaments, reflect His teachings every day of the remaining eleven months of each year.

Age of Reasoning

But Jesus said, Suffer little children and forbid them not to come to me, for of such is the kingdom of heaven. Matthew 19:14.

OH! TO SEE CHRISTMAS through the eyes of a four-year-old! The flashing sparkle in her dark brown eyes keeps time with the dance in her step. Afraid she'll miss even a flicker in the ever spinning kaleidoscope of Christmas pageantry, she glances from sight to colorful sight. "I can't wait for Christmas!" she whispers, then scampers off to watch another animated decoration.

At home, her fervor builds. She greets each guest at the door and rushes them to see the advent wreath, then the tree. With pride, she points to the lowest branches which she decorated all by herself. Although she is normally fearful to venture into the bedroom wing of the house alone at night, she runs fast to her room to retrieve her letter from Santa Claus. Caught in the spirit of the season, she is compelled to share her excitement.

While new adventures fill her days like pyrotechnics exploding in a Fourth of July sky, the repetition of old favorites soothingly cuddle her in teddy bear fashion. Let someone sit down, and she will crawl into his lap with her favorite Christmas story, "Read it to me!" she pleads demandingly.

Having heard the story of Rudolph so often, she reads right along and catches even the slightest attempt to condense the tale. She carefully studies each picture, always looking for something she might have missed before. "Rudolph is Santa's headlight," she concludes matter-of-factly.

In all of the times the story has been read to her, no one has ever made the comparison for her nor prompted her to that conclusion with taunting questions. It is an understanding she has reached on her own. And she is puzzled why such simple comprehension should amuse so many people.

Parents the world over smile when their offspring "say the darndest things."

Because children can always be counted upon to come forth with the unique, newspapers even send reporters out to ask them such questions as "what does Santa look like?" Now everyone knows what Santa looks like. Or does he, until he views the gift giver through very young eyes.

But the childish remarks most remembered are the ones that are the result of reasoning. Even if the reasoning is a bit faulty, it is those times when a youngster can transfer one piece of knowledge to another that makes us proud. Comparable to taking a first step on wobbly legs, such reasoning is the first step to great understanding. No wonder it is exciting. We all grow when we discover an age old truth for ourselves.

And so it is with the Christmas message. Like children, we can so easily get caught up in the hustle and bustle of the holidays. But when we learn to translate the overwhelmingly good feelings which come with the holy season into every day action throughout the new year, then we, too, have discovered Christmas for ourselves.

Let Me Hold You

And he took them up in his arms, put his hands upon them and blessed them. Mark 10:16.

THE TWO-YEAR-OLD SOMETIMES WEARS an impish grin, sometimes, a far away, pensive look. With such intensity in his eyes, both photographers and artists attempt to capture his expression in their work.

He likes the football team, the winning season, the enthusiasm in the air and the band. He thinks he wants to play in the band one day. He likes the parades. He likes the excitement. He likes the noise. Because of his fascination with all the hoopla, his mother took him to a pep rally at the high school stadium. With so much activity in a limited space, he watched it as if he were at a three-ring circus. He watched the cheerleaders, then the band, the mascot, the football players and the students. He pointed to each. He swayed to the music and he clapped his hands. He stomped his feet. In his own small way, he cheered.

As his adrenaline level began to drop, he held his arms up to his mom. "Let me hold you," he pleaded. Chuckling at his reversal of words, she picked him up. He lay his head on her shoulder and snuggled his face against her neck. Tired, comfortable, secure, he closed his eyes and drifted off amidst shouts of "Go, team, go!"

Always, we smile at the naïveté of the young. In the way they phrase their words, through their view of the surroundings, by their enthusiasm to see anew what we have taken for granted, we stand amused. And yet, in those very qualities so dear to childhood, we, too, can see anew.

Two thousand years ago, another little boy came into the world. Every December we celebrate his birth in song and story and hopefully, in deed. He, too, extended His arms and said, "Let me hold you."

But the Christ Child didn't confuse His words. He was born to hold the world in His hands. His invitation never ceases. His arms remain outstretched to anyone who reaches up. And when He holds us, He comforts us as surely as the mother cuddles her child.

Jesus Christ appreciated the presence of the very young. He placed His hands on their heads to bless them. He admonished anyone who would deny a child access to Him.

Some children are brats early on because their parents let them be. It is hard work to raise a child to become his own person, one that people, himself included, want to be around. Other children bring joy from the day they are born. Their zest for living never wanes. But all the children, the lovable and the not so likable, must be nurtured if they are to reach the potential within. That's why parents were invented, not just to conceive a child, but to lead a child to the person he can be. And the message of Christmas lies in that strong relationship between the parent and the offspring.

"Let me hold you" may be the cute confusion of words by a child who wants to be picked up. "Let me hold you" also bonds family. But the offer of the Christmas Babe, day in, day out, remains constant. "Let me hold you." His invitation is the gift of

Christmas. But to receive it, we must first accept it. He never thrusts it upon us. Like the child wanting to be picked up, we must reach up to Him. Like the mother reaching down to lift the child, we must also reach out to all His children.

Lots of Batteries

Suffer little children...to come unto me; for of such is the kingdom of Heaven. Matthew 9:14.

IN JULY, THE THREE-YEAR-OLD, dark brown ringlets circling her face, sat buckled in an air-conditioned car. Her child safety seat raised her high enough to see sun rays creating patterns on the hood. Fascinated by the glare, she turned to her mother and began a barrage of questions about the sun.

Why is it so hot? Why does it make the car shiny? Why can I still feel it inside the car? What color is it? Why is it so hard to look at? The mother tried her best to answer each in the onset of inquiries.

One question led to another until the child finally asked, "Who made the sun?"

The mother smiled at her very inquisitive daughter, dressed in a faded blue denim shorts set trimmed with bright red watermelon slices, and replied, "God made the sun."

With that answer, silence. They drove for a long time through the midday heat and the Atlanta traffic. Neither spoke as the mother focused on driving safely, and the child continued to watch the sun reflect off the hood of the car.

Almost home, the child turned to her mother once again and proclaimed, "God must have used a lot of batteries to make the sun so hot!"

Children know about batteries. Much of their small world runs on them. Grandparents, who want toys that children cuddle or drive on their own steam, find it difficult to purchase Christmas presents that don't require batteries. And, wise parents keep a large stock on hand. Inevitably, the favorite plaything runs down at the most inopportune time.

Batteries have been around for a long time, at least as long as I can remember. However, it seems that in the past few years, their use has multiplied. In fact, batteries have become so much a way of life now that I noticed the other day a business that sells nothing but batteries. The customer in the television commercial runs through a long Santa-like list of battery needs and the clerk keeps repeating, "We have that; we have that." And the Energizer Bunny that keeps on going and going has become a part of advertising lore. Yes, the battery symbolizes the times.

And thus we return to the Christmas in July story, to the child who envisions God using lots of batteries to run His world. At first, we smile at her innocence and faulty reasoning. And then we see, like Jesus admonishes us, she is the wise one. She will learn the Biblical renditions of the Christ Child's birth. She probably will portray a variety of characters in the nativity scene before she is grown.

However, without any instructions and only through her own intuition, she brings God, as a very real entity, into her own life. She doesn't relegate Him to Christmas Sunday or the manger. To her, He's a vital part of life as she knows it. And therein, lies the Christmas message.

Oh, we can sing, and we should, "Silent Night," "Away in the Manger," and "We Three Kings of Orient Are." The Christmas story begins our annual journey through the next year. But if we pack the message away with the ornaments, if we go on a spiritual diet after we consume the last cantata, if we consign our religious education to Sunday School only, then we didn't hear the story at all.

God is as real and as modern as any size battery. And when we invite Him to be an essential part of our everyday lives, He lasts much longer than any of our prize possessions. It seems so easy for the children and so difficult for us, to bring Christmas out of the past and let it direct all that we do and think each day. And yet, that is our charge.

Fast Asleep in a Box

And she brought forth her first born son, and wrapped him in swaddling clothes, and laid him in a manger; because there was no room for them in the inn. Luke 2:7.

IT WAS BABY'S SECOND Christmas; she had just celebrated her first birthday the month before. She delighted in the sights and sounds of the season. She stared at the colors and the glitter and the movement as if she were trying to absorb the swirling kaleidoscope before her eyes. She listened to the music and swayed. She tried to unwrap the presents and pull the ornaments off the tree.

Come Christmas morn, she joined her older brother and sister in the excitement of Santa Claus. At last, no one told her "no" as she pulled at the wrappings. Somehow, with permission, snatching bows soon lost its fascination. And so, Mother knelt to help her unwrap her gifts.

The child poked the doll, glanced at the book, pushed away the clothes. But, she claimed the boxes. She drove one around the living room floor like a toy car. She then turned it on top of her head like a hat and joined in with her own sweet giggle when everyone else laughed at her.

As Christmas morns tend to do, the older children moved to other rooms to play with their new toys. Mother started breakfast while Dad cleaned up the wrappings. And that's when he discovered his youngest, fast asleep, like Little Boy Blue, not under a haystack, but in the largest of the boxes.

We all like boxes. In this computer age, the whizzes love to make new files and place them in flat icon folders that resemble little boxes on the screen. One of the fastest growing retail businesses in the country is the one that offers a wide variety of boxes and shelves to organize our closets. Organization is supposed to simplify the hectic disorder we find ourselves in. For, if everything is kept neatly in its proper place, we can cope with it, can't we?

We Christians are as guilty as the rest of the world in trying to box up our faith. Some want to keep Jesus gift wrapped all year long. The trimmings, the music, the words, the good tidings make us feel warm inside. If only we could leave a covering of Christmas decorations over all over the world year round, we wouldn't have to deal with the ugliness that lies beneath.

Others of us want to keep God in a box of our own choosing up on a closet shelf. With such an arrangement, we then can pull Him out only when we want something. With a polishing rub, we can expect our three most fervent wishes granted as if He were a genie in a bottle.

Some want to box God into the rules found in His good book. If only we cross the t's and dot the i's of all the laws, then God will reward us. Yet, Jesus Himself chastised the Scribes and Pharisees for keeping the letter of the law but overlooking its spirit.

Like all good mothers, Mary must have wanted to keep her first born protectively swaddled for as long as she could. But according to the Bible, same chapter, Jesus grew "in wisdom and stature and favor with God and man." However, that growth troubled his parents because He was not where He was supposed to be. And thereafter, He troubled the religious establishment until its practitioners plotted to kill him.

For time and time again, Jesus said, "Thou shalt love the Lord thy God with all thy heart and with all thy soul and with all thy mind. This is the first and great commandment. And the second is like unto it, Thou shalt love they neighbor as thyself. On these two commandments, hang all the law and the prophets."

No longer are we commanded not to kill, not to steal, not to covet because God commands it. Rather we now refrain from such antisocial behavior because we love God and His children. We also seek the best for one another because we have encountered the power of real love. In marriage, we don't want our spouses to be faithful because they must according to moral law. Instead, we want them to be faithful because they love us so much they cannot consider a life without us. Love is so much more than an emotion. Love is the action we take to make room for everyone in the inn.

We love because He first loved us. The pagans created their deities in the image of man, a system that left the people unfulfilled. Yet when we try to box God in so we can hold onto Him to make the world less chaotic, we fall into the same trap of trying to recreate the Creator in our image. No matter what man may discover or thinks he discovers, we do not diminish God. We may hurt ourselves, but He is truly omnipotent and omnipresent. Yet as our awareness of God increases, so can our relationship with Him grow in like proportions. God cannot be put in a box. He cannot be contained in a pretty package. He cannot be used as a genie.

To carry the spirit of Christmas with us year round, we must first unwrap the baby Jesus and let Him grow up. We must sit at his feet and listen to his words. And because we are created in His image, and not He in ours, we must love as He loves.

What Do We Do with the Empty Bird's Nest?

Ye observe days and months, and times and years. Galatians 4:10.

TWO FRIENDS TALKED. "I hate to see Christmas decorations come down. Everything looks so bare at this time of the year," one said.

"Clean," said the other. "Everything looks so clean after we clear away Christmas."

I agree with them both. I love the Christmas season, not only the decking of the halls, but also the outpouring of kindness. I like the consideration many show others during this festive time. Even strangers greet strangers in a way they never do during the rest of the year. It's sad that we can't hold on to this generosity of spirit the whole year through. But I also like the promise of each new year. I, too, like the reflective time that comes when all the decorations are gone.

I enjoy traveling in the mountains in the wintertime for that very reason. Of course in the mountains, I like the newness of spring high on the hill, the coolness of summer, the color of autumn, but most of all I like the starkness of winter.

Outside my mountaintop window stands a lone tree, devoid of all trappings save a lone leaf, a bit of mistletoe and an abandoned bird's nest. Soon the solitary leaf will fall. Because Christmas has come and gone, the mistletoe will remain in this tree for another year. Yet, I wonder about the bird's nest. What happens to these woven wonders of straw after they have served the purpose for which they were carefully constructed? Do the birds strip and reuse parts or will it eventually fall like the leaf, thus allowing nature to recycle it?

Beyond the tree, I can see the rise and fall of the land as these old mountains roll from peaks to valleys. Lights blink like signals on distant summits. Smoke curls from chimneys. To see beyond the trees is the reason I come to the mountains in the winter.

After the deciduous trees flame, then drop their annual foliage, but before new life buds, the mountains take on a different look. No longer does the panorama of color, from spring green to fiery red, dominate the view; the strength of the mountains and of the people who choose to brave the elements year round become visible. They are no longer hidden by leafy curtains of many colors or hordes of city folk trying to glimpse nature at her spectacular best.

Likewise at this time of year, after Christmas, before the rush of the new year, newspapers review the top stories and reflect on those who made news. Businesses take inventory. Students take finals. Most of us, when all the decorations come down, look beyond the usual trappings of life and remember days gone by before we ever mark the clean pages of a new calendar of a new year. We, too, take stock. We, too, recall what we have learned. If not, we should.

We frequently tell our young people, "Just Say No!" Learning to turn down life's temptations is part of growing up. And from the time children learn through their play to imitate adults, they want to be grown. When one is young, waiting – waiting for Santa, waiting for the right time, waiting for life – seems impossible. But learning to wait is part of growing up, is part of the life we are living.

Likewise, learning to make wise choices is a lifelong experience. As we grow older, we begin to realize that we must not crowd our lives with too much busy work. Many worthwhile causes cry out for our time and attention. If we're not careful, we can let these demands camouflage living. With maturity, we learn to say "no" easily.

Yet over a lifetime of learning to say "no," we, if we're not careful, often forget how to say "yes." It becomes so easy to stay at home, to ignore the needs of others, to nurse our own complaints, to pull back into a comfortable shell and let the rest of the world pass us by, to live in the negative, to find fault in everyone and everything. And when we do, we forfeit the very life we clamored for as children.

A young mother, in chasing her toddler, comments on how fast time flies. A hospitalized friend muses about how slowly time moves when one is confined to bed. It is the same time, just different perspectives. They, like my two friends, who view this time of year differently, merely stand at different windows.

None of us knows what the new year will bring. But before the clutter takes over following the housecleaning after Christmas, let us pause and stare at the white pages of our calendar. What do we really want to do with each day? As we take pen in hand to record the upcoming events already crowding into our lives, how do we distinguish between what is really important and what merely passes the time? The leaf will fall and the mistletoe will grow for another year. But what do we do with the empty birds' nests in our own lives?

Dancing with the Bees

Let them praise his name in the dance: let them sing praises unto him with the timbrel and the harp. Psalms 149:3.

A TWO-YEAR OLD SAW a furry blue kitty in the toy store.

"Buy it, please," he begged in the same universal tone of children as they pass the candy at the grocer's checkout counter.

Mother declined the request, but took note of the longing in his eyes as he waved goodbye to this most unusual rendition of feline. She had told him about the blue fairy in "Pinocchio," but a blue cat?

However, when Christmas morning rolled around, he squealed with delight upon seeing his new friend lying amidst the tissue in the box from his parents. "Kitty," he named it as he squeezed it close to him.

Always the one for the gimmick, he laid the stuffed animal aside and took far more notice of the wind-up or battery operated toys that Santa and other members of the family had given him.

But when bedtime came, it was the blue cat that accompanied him under the covers. As he said his prayers, he gave thanks for his new companion; and after the "Amen," he thanked his mother again, this time with an extra tight hug. The cat was not only a toy he had wanted; evidently, he needed it, too.

Most other toys made their way into the toy chest, and eventually, the trash can. But he clung to the blue kitty cat until it was beyond washing and mending. He loved it to death. His parents always knew by his actions alone how very special this gift had been. But then, actions always speak louder than words.

Children aren't the only ones who often show better than tell. According to Steve Manning, staff naturalist with the Smithsonian Institute, bees, likewise, communicate through dance. "When the scout bee discovers a new source of pollen," he writes, "it returns to the hive and communicates its discovery in dance. The pattern of the dance tells the other bees which direction to fly, and the speed of the dance tells them how far."

He adds that the dance of the bees even has dialects. "Expert bee watchers can tell from its dance what part of the world a bee is from."

Dogs and cats, along with bees and children, certainly show their feelings, too. There is no doubt where owners stand with their pets.

However, we adults often tend to hid our deepest feelings. We teach our young to offer perfunctory thanks with the reminder, "What do you say when someone gives you a gift?" And we conscientiously write thank you notes and repeat grace at the table.

But do we really show gratitude? In our day to day living, many of our realities are not harsh, but these blessings we tend to take for granted. They are our rights. And if we remember to thank those around us for a kindness or even voice praise to God, do we really show appreciation by how we utilize our many blessings? I think not. If we did, our very environment would not be in danger. We have become so busy existing that we have forgotten how to live.

At this holy season, let us sing and dance with the psalmist. It is good to give thanks both with our words and our actions.

The Bells Are Still Jingling

I will sing with the spirit, and I will sing with the understanding, also. I Corinthians 14:15.

"JINGLE BELLS!" SHOUTED THE children when asked what song they would like to sing.

Two weeks after Christmas and they still wanted to sing the holiday song. And sing they did. "Dashing through the snow in a one horse open sleigh...Oh what fun it is to laugh and sing a sleighing song tonight...Jingle Bells, Jingle Bells, Jingle all the way..."

What a verse for South Georgia preschoolers to want to sing. Few of them probably have ever seen snow, much less a one-horse open sleigh. They would be at a loss if asked to define the words of this old favorite.

But it's the melody they enjoy and the feeling they want to re-capture. The tune sounds like bells ringing; and there is no other time, including a child's birthday, that is as exciting for a child as is Christmas. Midway into the first month of the new year, they want to go back. The very youngest want to return to the sights and sounds and wonders of the holy day.

They'll learn soon enough that life goes forward, that there is no going back. Growing up comes as we stack feelings on top of feelings, deeds on deeds, memories on memories.

Several days before the children's request, I caught the tail end of a request from Paul Harvey on the radio. He was looking for an analogy to "you can't unring a bell." The offering for the day was "you can't unbreak an egg." Harvey didn't think the latest suggestion cracked up to what he was looking for. It didn't have the same ring to it.

Think about it. A bell doesn't just ring. The resonance reverberates with an echoing effect that lingers both in the air and in our minds, like the children's memory of Christmas past.

'Tis true we can't unring it. If it is a mistake, we can't take it back, pretend it never happened. We can make restitution, apologize, redo.

And even if we like the sound, we shouldn't overdo it until it loses it charm. We are admonished to keep the spirit of Christmas year round, but if we tried to keep the trappings much longer, the colors would fade, the tree would lose its needles, and we would grow weary. The children don't know it yet, but part of the awe of Christmas comes in the renewal.

We can't unring the bell. But, like adhering to the message of Christmas 365 days a year, we can live it again and again and again.

Mo' Christmas

There is a lad here, which hath five barley loaves and two small fishes, but what are they among so many? John 6:9.

BEFITTING HIS NAME, THE toddler dressed as Sam-I-Am of Dr. Seuss fame for Halloween. "We had better dress him as his namesake this year because next year, he'll be old enough to decide what he wants to be," his mother said.

And so, she fashioned his garb of a pale yellow fringed gown, floppy red hat and sign proclaiming him Sam-I-Am. He loved the sign. He, like the character of book fame, carried it everywhere until it disintegrated. Not to be thwarted, he pulled and tugged and pulled and tugged until he pulled up the security warning sign in the front yard. "Mo' sign," he declared and he carried it around until Daddy pounded it all the way into the ground.

In the ever popular *Green Eggs and Ham*, Sam tries to get the grouch to share a favorite meal. The grouch will have none of it, "not in a house, not with a mouse, not on a boat, not with a goat." But Sam is persistent. And finally, the grouch tries the odd combination, likes it, and thanks Sam for not giving up.

Not really a Christmas story or is it? Soon after the toddler forfeited his second sign, he discovered cookies or at least the word for them. He's at that age. The world is full of treats. For the longest time, he's grunted and pointed for everything he's wanted. But recently, he's put the power of words to work for him.

He once asked for Mo' fish and received it. And from the time that he first asked and received a cookie from the cookie jar, he hasn't stopped. "Cookie...Mo' cookie...Cookie...Mo' cookie." Needless to say he likes to eat. And as much as he likes cookies, he could give the Cookie Monster of Sesame Street a run for his name.

Typical youngster, he wants, and he's persistent until he receives. Oh can he ever cram his mouth full of the delectable treat.

However, since he's still into naming objects, "more" or as he pronounces it, "Mo" is probably the abstract word he has made his own. Like most his age, he understands if he likes something – food, story, song, cuddles – he wants it repeated.

But he doesn't always gobble down seconds. With the second cookie, the Mo' one, he, especially if someone is holding him in her arms, extends the goodie toward the giver for a bite. Mo' means a cookie to share. The giver isn't always receptive to the offer because of the child's grimy hands. But the youngster always tries to give away Mo' cookie, or at least, part of it.

So why should it surprise us, after all the Christmas decorations were down, that he found a small ornament that had rolled under the couch. He retrieved and gave it to his mother. That's right, with the words, "Mo' Christmas."

According to the Biblical story of feeding the multitudes, a little boy gave Jesus all that he had, the five loaves and two fishes. And after the Master blessed it, He fed five thousand.

Critics over the centuries have tried to explain away this miracle. One such explanation claims that the crowd, when it witnessed the unselfishness of a child, opened their bags and shared what they, too, had brought.

To me, a mob of people generously sharing with one another is a far greater miracle than the image of the Master multiplying food. And yet, wanting to share is the miracle He works in us when we believe. In following in His footsteps, we share, not because He commands us, but rather because we want to. Our hearts have changed. That truly is a miracle. From the blessings that come with the sign, Mo' sign; fish, Mo' fish; cookie, Mo' cookie; Christmas, Mo' Christmas, we learn to give, not out of obligation, but rather from the heart.

The Joy of the Littlest of Angels

And the angel said unto them, Fear not: for behold, I bring you good tidings of great joy, which shall be to all people. Luke 2:10.

IT WAS A SMALL church, a chapel really. Outside, the weather was cold and dreary, but inside, warmth, not only from the heater, but also from the congeniality of the gathering crowd permeated the sanctuary. Before the choir sang its "Joy" cantata, the children presented their interpretation of the Christmas story.

To be assured a seat, we had arrived early. And it wasn't long until I found myself smiling at the littlest of angels.

Shortly after we were seated, she, with green eyes sparkling, skipped down the aisle with her filmy wings flapping on her back, but her unruly halo attached to a headband would not stay in place atop her auburn hair pulled tightly into a ponytail. She tried again and again to replace it, but even when the plastic band sat firmly on her head, the halo listed to one side as if it were a dingy with an unbalanced load.

Grouped with a host of angels, she sang as if she meant every word. And when it came time for her to recite her part, she did so without hesitation. She not only was well rehearsed in what to say, but also when to speak, a feat not matched by one of the older girls playing a Magi, who kept moving to the microphone out of turn.

As these children performed, I was immersed in a cascade of memories about our own children. They, too, had been in such productions. I could see our oldest, draped in blue to portray Mary, greeting us after the performance. "Did you see, I was part of the Christmas story tonight." And before our middle child took to the stage as an angel, he, garbed in a discarded, yellowed choir robe and tennis shoes, exclaimed, "I'm a cheap angel. My wings are made of coat hangers covered with silver garland." After the performance, he, too, believed. Our youngest, who loved uniforms, but hated costumes of all kinds, reluctantly served as the Santa in the kindergarten production. Refusing to wear padding and whiskers, he was the skinniest, most beardless Santa Claus ever seen. And I smiled again at the continuity of children reenacting the spirit of Christmas year after year.

After these present day children told and sang the story of that first Christmas 2000 years ago, they were ushered to the front row to watch the grown-ups, all dressed in red shirts and blouses, show them how to perform. And these children now seated were the epitome of how we want all children to behave appropriately at times such as these.

All, but the littlest of angels. Now free of that aggravating halo, she listened intently to the choir repeat the same story that the children had just told. As the choir harmonized with a lively song, the director began to clap and encouraged the now standing audience to join in. With great joy, the littlest of angels began to clap with the music. But the beat was just too much for her.

Within seconds, she was on her feet, in the aisle, dancing and swaying to the music. At that very moment, she was the embodiment of great joy, filled with good tidings. In the innocence of the littlest of angels, the baby lying in the manger on the altar was no longer a doll, but rather God Incarnate living among us.

"Joy to the World, the Lord is come..." the choir sang.

In the Biblical story, the angels end their visit to the shepherds by saying, "Glory to God on high and on earth peace, good will toward men."

Cellist Yo Yo Ma, in explaining the title of his album, "Joy and Peace," recorded with songwriter/singer Allison Krauss, said, "There is no joy without peace."

How true. At this year's holy season, we may not have freedom from war, nor freedom from fear with the weak economy, but the celebration of the birth of Christ can certainly bring us peace within our souls, and with that inner peace comes joy, great joy. And while we may not demonstrate that emotion bubbling within us like the littlest of angels, we, too, can know the great exhilaration that this child freely expressed, uninhibited by the mores and restraints that often limit us adults. However, such joy and peace can last far beyond the moment to enrich every day of the new year if we embrace it. And when we do, such joy becomes contagious, one to another.

Listen to the Child...

And Jesus called a little child unto him, and set him in the midst of them, and said, Verily I say unto you, Except ye be converted and become as little children, ye shall not enter the kingdom of Heaven. Matthew 18: 2-3.

MOONLIGHT REFLECTED ON THE waters of Hickory Creek when the two-year-old bounded up the stairs into the arms of his grandfather. "I saw deers! I saw deers!" exclaimed the child whose eyes, arms and feet danced with the excitement of the night's adventure. "I saw real deers!"

As his parents entered the private drive to the grandfather's home, they slowed at a clearing noted as a habitat for white-tail deer. Removing his seatbelt, they allowed the youngster to slip out of his car seat and stand by the window. When they spotted the animals in the headlights, they stopped and watched. And, the animals watched back.

Two years later, whenever they make the same drive, the child still searches for "real deers!" At this time of the year, he has already seen plenty of lighted, molded lawn and store ornaments in the shape of deer. However, he isn't looking for

Rudolph, Dasher, Dancer or any of the other famous reindeer of story and song. He always wants to see "real deers." Usually, he does.

At four now, he's also into Spider-man. He likes anything Spider-man - pjs, T-shirts, sheets, watches, action figures. His favorite, though, is the hand-me-down Spider-man costume that two of his older cousins have outgrown. He would wear it all the time if his Mother would let him. He marvels in amazement that the big kids parted with this treasure. "Can you believe it?" He says with awe. "They gave me their Spider-man suit!"

In yet another announcement, as he prances around in his blue and red costume, he acknowledges a difference. "I'm not a real Spider-man. I can't shoot spiderwebs from my hands. I can't climb walls. But, it's okay to pretend."

At the wise old age of four, this child recognizes first hand the difference between "real" and "pretend." And, he revels in both.

However, at this time of the year especially, it is a hard distinction for many supposedly grown-ups to make. Of course, we know "the reason for the season." Tears well in our eyes when we reread the Christmas story. Then we decorate some more, and complain about how much we have to do "to get ready."

To stop this conflict between "real" and "pretend," many advise eliminating all trappings. Focus only on the serious.

But listen to the child.

He can wear his pretend Spider-man costume while he seeks out the real deer.

Normally in perpetual motion, he can stand oh so still to keep the skittish wildlife close. He feels immense gratitude that his cousins were so generous and thoughtful. Yet, in some instinctive way, he also appreciates his ability to pretend.

Reread the Christmas story in all the gospels. It is full of trappings. A huge fiery star noticeably moving across the sky. Singing angels. Shepherds herding their sheep into town. Wise men bringing gifts. Don't forget the miracle of birth itself. Or, God's choice to live among us.

Christmas flourishes with all of the pageantry - music, drama, decorations, gifts, flowers, cards, good feelings - that our human minds can conceive to celebrate this great moment in history. After all, the ability to pretend is one of God's many great gifts to human beings because it teaches us how to be creators also. We can never match God's wonders, but we can share His creative spirit by being good stewards of His world, by appreciating His generosity, by finding ingenious ways to hallow His birth and life, by sharing our good fortune with all of His children.

The "real" Christmas does not ask us to discard our ability to pretend, to imagine. Instead, the "real" Christmas inspires us to live with its message in our hearts at all times. Celebrate Christmas by listening closely to the children. With the abandon of a child, delight in the holy observances. Conceive ways to do God's work, then do it. Treat others not only as we want to be treated, but also in the ways God wants us to treat others. With the enthusiasm of a child, hold firmly to the giving, loving, sharing spirit of Christmas all year long, year after year after year.

The New Year Babe

And Jesus increased in wisdom and stature, and in favour with God and man. Luke 2:52.

IT COMES DRAPED IN a diaper and a banner - the New Year Babe. Three hundred and sixty-five days later, it leaves an old man who has aged a lifetime in one short year.

The personification of time is vivid - the babe, full of hope and expectation; the sage, wise beyond his years. It is even a more fitting symbolism when we consider the wisdom which frequently comes out of the mouths of babes.

*****

The babe is a preschooler, inquisitive, active, happy. Eager to know, she pokes and pries into each little cranny just to see. It's a good way to get little fingers trapped. Likewise, she rushes headlong into bigger explorations. But she learns.

About six months ago, anxious to get out of the car after what must have seemed as an endless trip to North Georgia, she scrambled out the open door and fell flat on her face. It hurt. She cried. It also damaged one of her two front teeth, discoloring it, but not dislodging it.

Her parents have watched the tooth carefully and have tried ever harder to keep up with her fast pace. But as Babe ages, so grows her curiosity and her agility.

A couple of weeks ago, she took another spill, this time sprawling across the concrete drive; and of course, hitting the same little tooth. It bled. She cried again.

And then began the long watch to make certain an abscess doesn't form under the injured tooth. After a week passed, she'd tell anyone who listened that her tooth still hurt.

But the pain didn't slow her down. Her mother walked into the bedroom only to find the youngster jumping off the bed.

"Don't do that! You'll get hurt again!" exclaimed the mother.

The youngster smiled and climbed back on the bed. Covering her mouth with both hands, she prepared to jump again.

"What are you doing?" asked the mother.

"I'm holding my teeth in my mouth!" she mumbled through her fingers as she made a flying leap into her mother's arms.

*****

As the New Year approaches, may we leap boldly, full of all the hope and expectations of the young. But, may we also remember the lessons history has taught us. It is much more fun to learn new things than repeat the old class. We must also remember, as the new year comes only a week after Christmas, Jesus came to teach us how to live each new day in each new year.

A Restless Heart

Blessed are they which do hunger and thirst after righteousness: for they shall be filled. Matthew 5:6.

TWO MOTHERS, EACH PUSHING a shopping cart with a toddler in it, and each with an older sibling about eight or nine in tow, stopped at the grocery store bakery counter and spoke to a clerk. The two moms chatted as they waited. The little boys, like little boys are wont to do, began their stroll along the bakery counter. They pointed at cakes, cupcakes, pies and cookies. They looked at one another, bumped one another, and laughed like young friends do.

Then, they reached the doughnut display. The fun ended. Their whole bodies ached with longing. The onlooker could see it, not only in their faces and eyes, but also in their outspread hands on the glass and in their legs which they willed to stand still. If they could have crawled through the glass into the case, they would have.

An astute clerk eventually walked over and offered the boys their choice of a chocolate chip cookie or a sugar cookie with sprinkles. Both accepted the sugar cookie and thanked the clerk.

Then one whispered, "can I have one for my little brother?" He nodded over to the child in a cart. The clerk gave each a second cookie. Both thanked her again. Dutifully, they carried the second cookies to their siblings before taking a bite of their own. Thereafter, the moment of extreme longing was gone. The boys didn't wander back to the doughnut case. Another clerk delivered a birthday cake to each mom and the group moved on through the store. But if one ever wondered what the personification of deep longing looked like, they only had to watch those two at the doughnut case.

At varying times, we've all know extreme yearning, a sense that we might actually break apart if we don't obtain our momentary heart's desire. Like with the little boys, these passions for material things usually pass with time.

But C. S. Lewis, a 20th century British English professor who wrote books on Christianity, calls the longing that lingers, the one that will not depart, "an inconsolable longing for we know not what."

People everywhere seek to fill that sense of emptiness with things. And when the latest gadget doesn't make the ache disappear, we buy the newest, more recent version. I am reminded of a wealthy developer, who when asked why he kept grasping for more land, whispered, "I can't stop." The gift of a cookie wouldn't have tampered his longing; acquisition of more property didn't either. Such deep, internal longing does not go away with mere acquisitions.

Some also try to fill that longing with busyness. If we work long enough and hard enough to fall asleep at night, then we don't have to acknowledge any inner emptiness. Like Lady Macbeth, no matter how hard we scrub, "the spot" will not go away. For her the spot was guilt; for many, it is a craving that will not cease.

And some seek power. If everyone else will acknowledge their astuteness, their importance, their superiority, the interminable inner yearning will be soothed. Funny thing, we do not view our own purposes achieved by meeting the exorbitant needs of an egotist. The list of ways and means to eliminate this gnawing sensation within goes on and on.

United Methodist minister and author, Adam Hamilton, in "The Meaning of the Manger," writes, "But here's something I am absolutely certain of: there is nothing you or your family members will open on Christmas morning that will ultimately satisfy the deepest longings of your heart...Our hearts hunger to know that we are loved; that our lives have meaning and purpose; that we can be forgiven and find grace; that we are not alone; that there is always hope. We hunger to know that even death will not be the end of us; and we hunger for joy, and peace, goodness, and grace."

Looking for Abby P.

What man of you, having an hundred sheep, if he lose one of them, doth not leave the ninety and nine in the wilderness, and go after that which is lost, until he find it? And when he hath found it, he layeth it on his shoulders, rejoicing. And when he cometh home, he calleth together his friends and neighbors, saying unto them, Rejoice with me; for I have found my sheep which was lost. I say unto you, that likewise joy shall be in heaven over one sinner that repenteth, more than over ninety and nine just persons, which need no repentance. Luke 7:4-7.

MY HUSBAND AND I settled as comfortably as one can on a bale of hay in front of a roaring bonfire at the annual Christmas tree lighting ceremony at Vogel State Park on the second weekend in December. On this, the ninth year of Christmas fellowship and fun in the park, the largest crowd ever, estimated around 500, had descended on the festivities. While most were from neighboring Blairsville, some hailed from as far away as Texas and California. A dozen or more families were camping in the park and probably a like number had taken residence in the park cabins. Since this was our third year to attend the ceremony, we felt like old timers.

Rain had chased us away early on our first visit. Snow began to fall after the ceremonies on our second one. This time, the night air chilled us to the bone but we could see stars and a full moon in the sky.

The handbell choir had played a medley of Christmas tunes and the Young Family of Dahlonega was ready to take center stage on the truck bed pulled up to the park's ballfield. With a cup of hot apple cider or hot chocolate in everyone's hand, anticipation rippled across the crowd.

However, before any singing, one of the Young family members asked that Abby P. please come to the stage. "You have lost your family," he said. With smiles we all waited for a child to come forth. Although there was much milling around the rather small space filled to capacity with such a large crowd, no youngster ran to the stage. Rather, the new park manager stepped forward to announce that an eleven-year-old, blonde-haired girl wearing a purple coat was missing and that the entire park would be "locked down" until she was found.

At the announcement, several men moved toward the park rangers to see if they could assist with a search. After a prayer for the girl and her family, the rest of us were invited to enjoy the program. And we did, sort of. I love to hear the old familiar carols and the lively secular selections as much as anyone, but I found myself looking around for a girl in a purple coat.

Purple must have been the color of the year. It seemed as if almost every child that passed me that night was wearing a heavy jacket in shades ranging from dark pink to dark purple. But the ones I saw were either too young or too old to be the missing girl.

I also noticed how many of all ages were wearing hats resembling animals from penguins to bison. Most of us were wearing more traditional hats, scarves and hoods, but I saw quite an array of barnyard and zoo animals walking around atop people's heads.

And the program continued.

I kept waiting for a quick announcement that the girl had been found, that she had merely wandered away from her family. Or, that she and a friend had sneaked off to try to find a warmer, quieter place to sit and talk as preteens are wont to do. But no announcement was forthcoming. Because our youngest granddaughter is an eleven-year-old blonde, I could empathize with the missing girl's worried family.

We love to stay in Georgia State Parks, not only because they are one of the state's best resources, but also because we find them well maintained, safe havens. Kids ride their bicycles in the campgrounds. This annual outing should offer a fun festivity for people of all ages. And yet with a larger crowd than usual, there could have been someone who came, not for good, clean fun, but bent for mischief.

And the program continued.

Just before the final song and lighting of the tree, the emcee received a note that the girl had been found and she was "fine." No further details were forthcoming. I could hear the collective sigh of relief ripple across the crowd. I don't know that any of us realized that we had been holding our breaths.

With the announcement, the words of "Silent night, holy night, all is calm, all is bright..." took on new meaning. And the tree lights seemed to shine more brilliantly this year.

Since I've been home, I've contacted both the Vogel park office and *The North Georgia News* that covered the event. No one could or would share any further details on what happened other than she had wandered away, been found and was fine. Thank goodness.

Yet, I don't think I was the only person in that crowd who had experienced such uneasiness with the initial announcement.

Probably those who live in the area have filled one another in on the details, but I don't have access to that gossip.

Even with the uneasy feeling that came over me while the child was missing, I'm glad I attended this annual event. Although the landscapes differ between the North Georgia mountains and the flat, black land of Dallas, Texas, where I grew up, finding pleasure in simple scenes prompted numerous happy memories of my childhood Christmases.

A lot of people put in hours of work to set up such an occasion. However, other than microphones, amplification of sound and electric tree lights, this celebration was free of technology. There were no flashing lights, loud noises, constant communications, interruptions that govern so much of modern life. Come to think of it, I didn't see a cellphone except those used to take pictures of one another.

Yet, the concern for a missing child sweeping across the crowd reminded me of the greater messages arising from Christmas, those about loving one another, about being our brother's keeper, about seeking the one lost while 99 were safe in the fold.

Green Is Her Favorite Color

*And this shall be a sign unto you...*Luke 2:12.

THE FAMILY DID NOT shop for a Christmas tree together nor did they go to the woods to chop one down. Those were scenes from storybooks. Dad brought theirs home from work. But as with every Christmas tree, once decorated, it was beautiful. Multicolored lights in red, blue, green, yellow, and purple encircled the evergreen. Helping to hang the ornaments - including the two she had made from jar lids at Sunday School - plus throwing slivers of silver called icicles on the low branches - made it especially wondrous to the four-year-old.

The whole month of December, Advent time, had brought new surprises each day. Everyone around her seemed to live in a constant state of anticipation, of joy, of kindness. And the Christmas music, "the song in the air," echoed everywhere. Although she was too young to put her feelings into words, she loved these times, and the good feelings stayed with her all month long.

Clad in her new Sunday best, a forest green velveteen dress with puffed sleeves and a small tatted ecru collar, she sat under the Christmas tree, almost the same color as her dress. As the year was winding down, all of the presents, including this new dress made by her mother, once under the tree, had been opened and put to use. The needles from this once live tree fell with a touch. The child scooped up fallen needles and let them sift through her tiny fingers from one hand to the other.

After watching her only child sit mesmerized by the discards soon to be vacuumed away, Mother seated herself by the little girl and asked, "What are you thinking?"

Without moving her eyes from the prickly needles, the child asked, "Why does Christmas have to end?"

The mother also picked up a handful of needles before responding. "Do you want more presents?"

The child, almost in tears, shook her head. "I got lots of presents. Books for you to read to me, coloring books and a new box of crayons, paper dolls, a new tea set, and new dresses for me and my doll." She ran the back of her hand over her dress and smiled. "It feels good."

Mother pulled the child into her lap and hugged her. "What do you like most about Christmas?"

The child looked at the needles in her hand. "I like the church songs."

"Christmas carols," Mother whispered.

"I like making Jesus a birthday cake. I like that everyone seems nicer. I like that everything feels good like my dress."

Mother kissed the top of her head.

The girl wiped the needles from her hands. "I don't like the tree falling apart. You've taken off all the pretties. What happens now?"

"This tree has served its purpose for us. Next year, we'll get a new tree. But while we'll throw this tree away, you can keep all of your good feelings about Christmas."

"How?" The child asked.

Mother said, "Every time you see an evergreen tree like this one, a tree that doesn't lose its leaves in autumn, one that remains green all year, let it remind you of all of these good feelings and know they will come again and again, each time you share with others. In fact, why don't you let the color green remind you to keep the Christmas spirit year round by doing something special for someone. Do it often."

The girl turned and hugged her mother.

Christmas never has to end.

Poinsettia

He is risen...Mark 16:6.

A CHRISTMAS PRESENT CAME wrapped in shiny green paper, tied up with a big red bow. More than a dozen flame red blossoms blazed at the top of slender green stalks covered with leaves of matching green color. Poinsettia – the special Christmas flower.

With the occasion, it was moved from dining table to coffee table, adding fiery beauty to every corner in which it was set. It was more than gaudy decoration; it was alive.

The holidays passed; the tree came down; the New Year came in; and the poinsettia bloomed and bloomed throughout winter – always a contrast of warm color against the bleakness of winter.

When spring arrived, the poinsettia was removed from its pot and planted in a flowerbed along side the house. The sun warmed it; the gentle rains nourished it and it grew from house-plant to bush – strong, straight, summer green.

As autumn's chill painted the soon-to-fall leaves brilliant gold and orange, the tips of the poinsettia once again burnished with red. Each day, new red spread across the plant's top leaves. A spectacular sight: it was enough to make every passerby stop and wonder.

The owner, proud of this magnificent blooming flower, intended to cover, to protect it if the frost of winter even headed as far south as this valley. But a rare freeze sneaked in like a thief and stole away the bright colors, leaving only a limp, dull skeleton of sticks. The withering continued all season long – a mute testimony to a sad death.

With the coming of the second spring, the dead stalks were pruned away, but the roots were left to rot away, thus enriching the soil. Once again, the sun shone warm and gentle, nourishing rains fell.

And lo – new green sprouted from the almost forgotten roots. What once appeared dead is now alive.

Easter.

Postscript: this once small plant eventually grew as tall as the house and whoever resides in the abode is free to cut poinsettias blossoms to make a centerpiece for the Christmas dinner table.

She Liked Act Two Better

Fear not for behold, I bring you good tidings of great joy which shall be to all people. For unto you is born this day in the city of David a Savior which is Christ the Lord. Luke 2:10-11.

SHE WAS THE LITTLEST angel in the Easter pageant.

One of only three children in the entire production, the little girl with blonde, curly hair was costumed in pink gauze to portray a nativity cherub. With sparkling halo and rustling wings, she knew she looked the part, but she felt dwarfed by the adults rushing here and there on stage.

A tall, stately brunette, draped in purple, was the Angel of Death. Dressed in black, the mourners writhed with weeping. And men who looked like giants to her stomped around in armored plate and pushed and shoved a man whose face bled from a crown of thorns. She wanted to tell him to hit back.

The little girl covered her ears when the cymbals clashed and the crescendo of the orchestra swelled with the drama of the moment; the stage lights flashed like lightning in a thunderstorm.

It was scary. She didn't like the first part of the play at all.

She didn't understand. She was supposed to be the Christmas angel. And to her, Christmas was a happy, joyous time full of presents and laughter and carols and bright shining lights. In this play, everything was dark and gloomy.

Her only appearance on stage came during a flashback. As she hovered over the holy family, it was she who accepted the Wise Man's gift of myrrh. But while she smiled on the Babe lying in the manger, the Angel of Death snatched the present from her young hands and flew across the stage to stand in the shadow of a cross. They had practiced the scene again and again, but the suddenness of the woman's action always took the youngster by surprise. And, she would stare at her empty hands.

Although she didn't return to the stage until the finale, she liked Act Two better. An aura of white light surrounded everything and everybody. A hush settled on stage and people spoke in whispers. The fragrance of fresh flowers filled the air, but best of all, the man who had been so mistreated earlier dominated every scene.

He was so gentle, so kind and when he turned from the audience and glanced back stage, he winked at her. She wanted to run to him, climb in his lap and give him a hug. He made her feel good.

The drama definitely wasn't a Christmas story. There were no gift-wrapped presents, no twinkling star, no decorated tree. Although she still didn't understand, she knew deep in her heart, it was better.

When the curtain rose for the finale, even though it wasn't the way they had practiced it, she ran center stage and put her hand in his as they took their bows. He smiled at her and she forgot all the horrors of Act One.

Years later, long after the cherub grew up, she came to realize that without Easter, there would be no Christmas. The gift God gave mankind at Easter also gave purpose to Christmas.

For on that night long ago in Bethlehem, it was more than just one new life that the angels sang about. It was also the beginning of a new kind of life.

"Fear not: for behold I bring you good tidings of great joy which shall be to all people. For unto you is born this day in the city of David, a Savior which is Christ the Lord."

Acknowledgments

TO BOB, MY HUSBAND, thank you for believing that I can do anything and everything, from driving car pools to out-of-town swim meets to writing weekly columns. You have always been my strongest advocate, editor, critic. Thank you. I love you.

To our children, Erin Denty Boyd, Eric Denty and Lowry Denty, thank you for being you. You were my first inspiration, now you are my friends and editors. You have shown me how wide a mother's love can reach.

To our children's spouses, Amy Monroe Denty, Cheree Brazzeal Denty, and David Boyd, thank you for loving our children, for establishing Christian homes for your own children, my grandchildren, and for becoming my friend.

To our first grandchild, Erica Boyd, thank you for sharing your artistic talents for this book. Your "angel in tennis shoes" adorning the cover invites the reader to pick up this little volume and peruse.

To all our grandchildren, Erica, Jordan and Mary Margaret Boyd, RED and Sam Denty, Jay and Ansley Denty, thank you for being yourself. You inspire me. I love being Marnie.

To the nieces and nephews who also inspired columns now in this book, thank you for your keen insights when you were young.

To all the other children and young-at-heart adults, both those I have known and those I have watched from afar, thank you for leading us to messages from God.

To Dink NeSmith, co-owner of Community Newspapers Inc., thank you for your support of me and my entire family in all of our endeavors. You made me believe that my Christmas columns deserved a wider audience.

To Elliott Brack, thank you for asking me to write a Christmas editorial, "Angel in Tennis Shoes," years ago.

To friends, Sandra Denty, Linda Eckle, Pat Nix, and Jackie Dekle, thank you for sharing with me a love for reading. I love discussing books and writing with each of you. You are an inspiration to me.

To the publishers at New Harbor Press, thank you for making this book, this collection of devotionals, come alive.

To the late Pete Bailey, thank you for inviting me to try my hand at writing columns over a half century ago. When I was hesitant about a weekly deadline, you said, "If you don't try, how will you ever know." I quickly learned that I work best with deadlines. Neither of us ever dreamed it would lead to the release of this book.

To my parents, the late Ruth and J. D. Lowry, thank you for teaching me to love reading and writing by being story tellers who loved to read and write. You also taught me how to nurture a grateful heart.

To the readers, especially those who have asked for a collection of my columns and those who told me that I opened their ears to the words of their own children, thank you for reading my words year after year, for telling me how this message or that one has touched you, and for asking for more. Writers of every genre appreciate readers; I am wonderstruck by your continued support.

Thanks be to God for leading me to tune into His messages uttered by the young. Let this collection of devotions stand as testimony to my belief in God and in the possibility that the meaning of Christmas can stay with us every day of every year. Christmas never has to end. May God bless this witness to His Glory.

CPSIA information can be obtained
at www.ICGtesting.com
Printed in the USA
BVHW051414061221
623331BV00016B/806

9 781633 574106